Job Search Workbook

a companion to
99 Minutes to
Your Ideal Job

ALSO BY William T. Mangum

99 Minutes to Your Ideal Job

Published by John Wiley & Sons, 1995
Professional, Reference and Trade Group
605 Third Avenue, New York, NY 10158-0012
New York, Chichester, Brisbane, Toronto, Singapore
ISBN 0471 111 26-0

Job Search Workbook

a companion to
99 Minutes to Your Ideal Job

by

William T. Mangum
Thomas Mangum Company

This publication is designed to provide information in regard to the subject matter covered. Although the Author has researched all sources to insure accuracy and completeness of the information contained in this book, we assume no responsibilities for errors, omissions, inaccuracies or any other inconsistencies herein. Any mistake or slights regarding people or organizations is unintentional. It is sold with the understanding that the publisher is not engaged in rendering legal, accounting, or other professional service. If legal advice or other expert assistance is required, the services of a competent professional person should be sought.

(Partially taken from the Declaration of Principles jointly adopted by a Committee of the American Bar Association and a Committee of Publishers.)

10 9 8 7 6 5 4 3 2 1

ISBN 1-881474-04-6
Library of Congress Cataloging Card Number—95-060261

Mangum, William T. 1931–

    Job Search Workbook

    Bibliographical references
    1. Job hunting - United States
    2. Job search - United States
    3. Career change and development - United States

TMI Publications • P.O. Box 50001, Pasadena, CA 91115-0001

Book and modified cover design by Ernest Weckbaugh, Casa Graphics, Inc.
Cover design by John Wiley & Sons
Printed in the United States of America

To all individuals who struggle

with the task of getting

a job search started,

organized, and

executed.

This work book is dedicated to the task
of making job hunting as effective and
simple as possible in an increasingly
competitive, complex and
constantly changing
business world.

Acknowledgments

The Job Search Workbook has been developed from many sources and particularly nourished by hundreds of job survey respondents and potential executive search candidates—all part of the thousands of job seekers talked to in the last several years who have expressed their trials, tribulations and successes regarding their job search. I am grateful to all of you for sharing your experiences and job journeys. To all involved in the hiring process—hiring managers, human resource and employment managers, job hunters and placement industry specialists, a very special thank you for your contributions.

Thanks to Carolyn Carter, a most able associate who labored through manuscript preparation and typing; Mary Fiorenza for her most able editing, Jan Freibergs and Maria Mangum for edit review, and Ernie and Patty Weckbaugh of Casa Graphics, Inc., for design, layout, computer typesetting and final editing.

To you, the reader, a thank you for any contribution you may care to make to future revisions to the Job Search Workbook. Your success can help others in their job search efforts, particularly where you find certain techniques, approaches and tools that worked for you that could be helpful to others. Mail or fax your response using the Recommendation/Information Update sheet provided on the last page of the workbook.

Send to: TMI Publications
         P.O. Box 50001
         Pasadena, CA 91115-0001
         or fax to 818 / 568-0638

Table of Contents

Part 1   1   TOOLS*

Starting Your Job Search: Tools* to Help You Get Organized

- Job Search Model   1
- 52 Questions to Ask Yourself   2
  - Personal Assessment Checklist   4   ✓
- Reviewing the 9-Step Job Search Process   11
- Completing the 11-Step Job Search Plan   13 ✓
- Setting Schedules and Making Plans   15
- Developing a List of Target Companies to Contact   15
  - Working All Effective Job Opportunity Sources   16
  - Sample Target List of Companies   17 -S-

Part 2   19

Gaining Employer Interest: How to Make Contact, Build Relationships and Interview Successfully

- Finding a Job Opportunity through Target Companies,   19
  Inquiry/Information Calls and Networking
  - A Behind-the-Scenes Job Opportunity   20
- Matching Qualifications to Employer Need   22
  - Sample Successful Cover Letter   25 -S-
  - Sample Winning Resumé   26 -S-
- A Winning Interview: Preparation and Effective
  Presentation   27
  - Questions to Ask Employers   28
    21 "Questions to Ask" Checklist   29 ✓
  - Employer Questions You May Be Asked   31
  - Other Ways to Gather Employer Information   32
- Providing and Prepping Your References   32
- Sample Follow-up Letter to Prospective Employer   34 -S-

Part 3   35

Evaluating, Negotiating, and Closing the Job Offer

---

*Working Tool Symbols
✓ (Checklist)   -S- (Sample)   -W- (Work sheet)   ❄ (Organizer)

● Job Search Success: An Offer Letter   35, 36   -S-
● Evaluating a Job Offer   37
   • Job Offer Items Category list   37
   • 17 Questions to Help You Evaluate a Job Offer   38   ✓
● Negotiating the Offer   39
   • Sample Successful Offer Negotiation Letter   41   -S-
   • Sample Amended "Employer Offer" Letter   42   -S-

Part 4   43   ✓

Starting Your New Job Right: 26 Suggestions

Appendixes: Checklists, Samples and Work Sheets

Appendix 1:   **Sample Organizational Tools**   47

Exhibit 1.A   Initial Job Search Activity Schedule:
              Week 1 Schedule and Checklist   50   ✓
Exhibit 1.B   Weekly Job Search Schedule and
              Checklist   54   ✓
Exhibit 1.C   Contacts Work Sheet: All Sources   57   -W-
Exhibit 1.D   Individual Job Source Work Sheet   58   -W-
Exhibit 1.E   Target Company Work Sheet   59   -W-
Exhibit 1.F   Telephone Call Prompt Checklist   60   ✓
Exhibit l.G   Telephone and Networking Work Sheet   -W-
              Organizer   64   ✽
Exhibit l.H   Interview Preparation Checklist   66   ✓
Exhibit 1.I   Master Organizer Overview Work Sheet   70   -W-
                                                ✽

Appendix 2:   **Cover Letter Samples**   71   -S-

Appendix 3:   **Resumé Samples**   77   -S-

Appendix 4:   **99 Employer Questions You May Be Asked:**   83   ✓
                 Checklist

Appendix 5:   **56 Potential Job Offer Items Work Sheet**   95   -W-

Appendix 6:   **Job Source Information List**   103
                 Reminder — Job Sources Available   114
                 Recommendation / Information Update   115

Introduction

This *Job Search Workbook* provides practical materials you can use in your job search and a model you can follow. The Job Search Model presented here follows the path taken by Ted Smith, a manager who had a good job, but who wanted a more challenging and rewarding position that offered greater potential for growth.[1]

This workbook is a companion to *99 Minutes To Your Ideal Job* (New York: John Wiley & Sons, 1994). You can use the workbook on its own, but you will gain more job search power by combining the tools you find here with the more detailed insights you will gain from reading — and applying — *99 Minutes*.

Both books are based on my thirty years of daily job market experience as an executive search consultant and search company president. The workbook is extensively drawn from the national job-hunter surveys used for *99 Minutes* and the many questions asked by thousands of job hunters seeking job-search help. It provides day-to-day working tools, and *99 Minutes* gives you the vital up-to-date information, methods, and techniques you need for your job search, the 99-Minute Formula, and the four new job hunting guides, all developed to help you . . .

- Get organized and started
- Get to know the job market and job-search process
- Analyze your job and personal strengths

---

[1] All names in this workbook, with the exception of John E. Smith, are fictitious to protect the privacy of the individuals involved.

- Research potential employers and develop effective job-source leads and opportunities
- Develop and execute your own job-search plan
- Market and sell yourself
- Gain employer interest
- Follow up and know how to close the interview
- Negotiate and close a winning job offer.

In my work with various companies, I have been involved with a gamut of industry and job levels, and have been recognized as one of the leading executive-search consultants and listed in *Career Makers: America's Top 100 Executive Recruiters*. I wrote *99 Minutes to Your Ideal Job* and developed this accompanying workbook to help people like you find the job they want in today's dramatically changed and often difficult job market.

As president of the Thomas Mangum Company, a nationwide executive-search company based in California, I have been fortunate to work with many thousands of job hunters and hundreds of employers. I have learned something from each of them. In addition, our firm has conducted surveys to keep abreast of changes in the job market. The surveys and questions have helped greatly in developing the schedules, work sheets, samples, checklists, and other tools you will find in the following pages. Use them to jump-start your trip to finding your ideal job.

Good job hunting! And the best of success in getting started in your new job.

William Mangum

1

Starting Your Job Search: Tools to Help You Get Organized

Job Search Model[1]

Ted Smith treated his job hunt as if he were a lawyer investigating a crucial legal case. He wanted the facts and all the information required to win. He knew when he started out, it wasn't going to be easy. He devised a job-search strategy, planned each step, worked with a schedule to make sure he executed his plan, and followed through. Ted was an excellent Marketing Manager, interested in finding a better position while currently employed. In his quest for the ideal job he investigated every angle of the job-search process and the job market. **His job search was successful in obtaining an offer and a counter-offer, and I am going to show you what he did so you can use his case as a guide to structure your own job search.**

The major steps Ted completed are described here in this work-book. I have also included samples to show you Ted's progress. In addition, you'll find other key steps, checklists and work sheets to help you in your job-search campaign. Use this workbook, follow Ted's path, and study the complete job-search campaign outline. You may want to begin by reviewing the guidelines for achieving success in Chapter 13 of *99 Minutes To Your Ideal Job* (hereafter referred to as *99 Minutes*).

Ted got his job search started using some basic organizational tools. You'll find examples of these in Appendix 1—work sheets, schedule, checklists, etc. You may find it useful at this point to review Chapter 5 in *99 Minutes*, "Taking Charge of Your Job Search."

---

[1]Model developed from individuals' job search with fictitious names and addresses used for confidentiality of individuals and companies.

Ted then completed a Personal Assessment Checklist similar to the one that follows. His next steps included a review of the job search process, developing and executing a job-search plan, developing and working various job sources, and developing a target list of employers to contact. After completing his organization, research and sourcing, target-company list, and other recommended steps, he began his presentation efforts by writing an initial rough draft cover letter and resumé. As his job sourcing and information gathering progressed, he wrote his initial resumé and cover letter tailored to employer needs. He focused his presentation efforts on gaining employer interest through *effective* presentation (using calls, contacts, and cover letters/resumés tailored to specific employers and specific individuals). He then worked on effective interviewing techniques, and what was required for evaluating, negotiating, and closing the job offer. All of these individual steps are covered in *99 Minutes* with checklists, samples, and work sheets on each step provided in this workbook.

52 Questions to Ask Yourself

The Personal Assessment Checklist will help you look at yourself and the job-search activities you have planned. The checklist can help you get your job search started or restarted if you are struggling with an ongoing job-search effort. If you have already started your search, it will be helpful in assessing your activities to date.

Ted found from his personal assessment that he needed to broaden his search efforts to more nontraditional job-search sources and techniques. He worked on developing an *effective* target-company list and on honing his networking skills. Additionally, he worked on his techniques of data gathering and inquiry calling. He realized that as he developed these skills, he would obtain vital information that would help him enhance his ability to interest prospective employers.

In working the checklist, rate yourself in each area. If you rate less than excellent to above average, pinpoint the problem and correct it. That is how you will succeed in today's job market.

Keep in mind your evaluation should be based on as much input as you can possibly derive from employers, associates, and others. Also remember that the ratings of employers and your immediate superior(s) can vary from employer to employer and within a company. It is important to consider the source of the evaluation and how that individual's positon may affect the rating. As an example, an adequate or above-average evaluation of your skills by a colleague may not be considered adequate or above average by a superior.

As you complete the following questionnaire, check off the items completed and record your ranking for each item. When finished, review the questionnaire to see if a single-key item or overall pattern emerges as an area you need to work on, such as: presentation skills, nontraditional job-search methods, marketing skills, effective job-source utilization, etc. You can use the ranking scale shown to rate your responses from excellent to poor.

52 Questions to Ask Yourself: Personal Assessment Checklist

Ranking Scale

Excellent or thorough = 4
Above average, up-to-date, or yes = 3
Average or room for improvement = 2
Poor, needs major improvement or no = 1

Check item completed. ✔

Indicate your ranking. (1, 2, 3, 4)

___ 1. Your overall presentation: verbal, written and personal(VWP). (See chapter 9 in *99 Minutes*) _____

___ 2. Your verbal presentation:
introduction _____
telephone presentation _____
interview skills _____
tone of voice _____

___ 3. Your written presentation:
resumé _____
cover letter _____
follow-up letters _____

___ 4. Your personal presentation:
dress _____
style _____
neatness/grooming _____
attitude/demeanor _____
approach (friendly, aloof, cold, etc.) _____

___ 5. Your nonverbal presentation:
body language _____
facial expressions _____

___ 6. Your overall approach:
Does it show a positive attitude? _____
Is it assertive without being overbearing? _____

___ 7. Are you working to polish your image by
        planning and practicing your presentation skills?
          phone (verbal)   _____
          resumé (written)   _____
          interview (personal)   _____

___ 8. Your work skills as they relate to today's
        employer needs.   _____

___ 9. Your education and additional training:
          education   _____
          additional training   _____

___ 10. Your experience and credentials:
          experience   _____
          credentials   _____

___ 11. Your knowledge of:
          the job market   _____
          what's happening in your
          areas of interest and skill   _____

___ 12. How effective is your approach with:
          companies   _____
          hiring managers   _____
          human resources management   _____
          employment personnel   _____
          others in your search   _____
          networked individuals   _____

___ 13. Your search plan:
          Is it detailed?   _____
          Is it comprehensive in conception/scope?   _____
          Is it completed?   _____

___ 14. Your target list:
          Is it on target for your skills/experience?   _____
          Is it comprehensive covering all areas
          related to your career field, capabilities,
          experience and skills?   _____

___ 15. Understanding and application of the job-search
        process:

Have you worked it effectively?   _____

___ 16. Job Sources:
Have you listed and worked all known
sources?   _____
Have you recently developed new ones?   _____
Are you searching out more possibilities?   _____

___ 17. Marketing yourself to find opportunities:
Are you being aggressive and assertive?   _____
(Are you passive and do you rely on
others to do this work for you? If so,
ask yourself why.)

___ 18. Time and effort applied to your search:
part-time, if employed   _____
full-time, if unemployed   _____

___ 19. Networking:
Do you have a systematic plan?   _____
Are you following up on your network
and company contacts?   _____

___ 20. Are you contacting companies with:
introductory calls   _____
inquiry calls   _____
hiring manager calls   _____
third-party introductions   _____
direct contact/applications to specific
named individuals   _____

___ 21. Are you making cold calls to develop/expand
your network and your potential employer
possibilities?   _____

___ 22. Are you attending meetings and rubbing elbows
with managers of companies where you want to
work as well as with people who can lead you
to them?   _____

___ 23. Job objectives:
Do employers consider them realistic?   _____
Do they result in employer interest?   _____
Do they result in job offers?   _____

___ 24. Have you been or are you upgrading your skills?   _____

___ 25. Are you matching your skills/experience to
employer needs (PEG Matching)? See Chapter 9
in *99 Minutes*.   _____

___ 26. Are you using nontraditional as well as
traditional job-search techniques and
sources (TNT). See Chapter 9 in *99 Minutes*.   _____

___ 27. Are you working the:
behind-the-scenes job market   _____
hidden job market   _____

___ 28. Are you working to discover jobs before they
formally exist that are in the early stages
of the employer job-opening and recruitment
process? See Chapter 8 in *99 Minutes*.   _____

___ 29. Are you listening enough (to potential
employers, network contacts and others)?   _____

___ 30. Are you providing too much detail in phone
calls and interviews that burden, overwhelm
and turn off the employer (i.e., talking too
much)?   _____

___ 31. Are you helpful to others in your job search
and related activities?   _____

___ 32. Are you seeking help from experienced
professionals in your job-search efforts?   _____

___ 33. Are you working all sources of job
opportunities that can lead to full-time
work such as:
temporary agencies   _____
part-time work   _____
consulting   _____
entrepreneurism   _____
interim assignments   _____

___ 34. Are you participating in various groups such as
         community support groups   _____
         professional associations   _____
         other associations   _____
         nonprofit organizations   _____
         Forty Plus   _____
         self-help groups   _____

___ 35. Are you willing to relocate?   _____

___ 36. Have you worked outplacement services to
maximum value?   _____

___ 37. Are you primarily just *working the visible
job market* (visible meaning the last four
steps of the job-opening and recruitment
process)? If so, you are missing over half the
potential job opportunities available. See
Chapter 8 of *99 Minutes.*   _____

___ 38. Are you getting input and feedback from potential
employers and from your interviews?   _____

___ 39. Are you aware of the interests of the potential
employer, hiring managers and human resource
executives involved in the hiring process?   _____

___ 40. Are you reading:
         job-market articles   _____
         self-help books   _____
         relevant professional and/or trade journals   _____

___ 41. What is your overall investment (time and money)
in learning how to improve you job-search effort?
         courses to improve skills   _____
         books on job hunting and the job-search
         process (give yourself credit for *this* book!)   _____
         counselors, consultants, self-help groups   _____

___ 42. In your networking have you contacted:
         leaders, college professors, and others
         in your career field or industry?   _____

authors and leads from relevant articles in trade, professional, technical or other publications? _____

___ 43. Have you assessed nonwork-related skill and knowledge areas for applicability to job or business opportunities (hobbies and volunteer activities, for example)? _____

___ 44. Are you asking people in your areas of interest questions such as—what are the latest changes and where is the field headed? (Is it growing, stagnant or shrinking?) _____

___ 45. Are you conducting a mini-survey of employers regarding professional areas of interest, product development, products, services, market research, and so on? This will develop interest and provide employers an introduction to your skills and talents for potential opportunities. _____

___ 46. Have you asked for assistance from groups that provide job-search help in your field or from groups in related fields (technical, professional, managerial, nonprofit, and others) or in possible recareering areas? _____

___ 47. Have you spent time studying the companies you are contacting including those on your target-company list? _____

___ 48. Have you created a job assistance group to help you and others expand your horizons and contacts (i.e., having an expert speaker on the job market and market issues, placements specialist, local employers)? _____

___ 49. Have you asked someone, preferably a professional, to be a job-search mentor to work with you? _____

___ 50. Have you approached employers, hiring managers, and professionals in your field to gather information on business issues, industry and industry association or trade matters? (You can later utilize these as a job prospect or lead.)   _____

___ 51. If you have experienced discrimination, are you handling it in a positive manner?   _____

___ 52. Are you working the job-placement industry effectively as to:

       job opportunities available   _____
       developing job opportunities   _____
       gaining leads and prospects   _____
       obtaining job-market information   _____
       utilizing help in your self-assessment
       process   _____

Reviewing the 9-Step Job-Search Process*[1]

As Ted worked the job-search process, he read up on the job market and what was required for a successful job search. He talked with various employers, human resource managers, and people in the placement industry to bring himself up-to-date on the job market, particularly in his areas of skill, experience and interest. **If you review the following Job-Search Process, as Ted did, you will save yourself a lot of time and effort.** (Chapter numbers refer to *99 Minutes to Your Ideal Job.*[1])

The Job-Search Process

1. The decision. It may be made voluntarily or involuntarily. In any case choose your time frame if you can, keep your cool, and master the job-search process to your benefit. Develop a job-search plan tailored to you and the job-market segments in which you must work. Use new approaches like the 99-Minute Formula and New Guides. (See Chapter 9 and 10.)

2. Finding a job. Getting a job search started and organized (developing a format, plan, action agenda, and setting a work schedule that includes goals and objectives). (See Chapters 4 through 8.)

3. Becoming informed. Learn all you can about the job market and yourself. In organizing your search, develop a multidirectional effort in order to learn what jobs are available on the surface of the market, behind the scenes, and in the hidden job market. Endeavor to research and source all job opportunities and possible opportunities in your area of interest. Learn the various methods of developing job opportunities. (See Chapters 3, 8 and 10.) You will also want to review your skills, experience, capabilities and talent. (See "Getting To Know Yourself" in Chapter 6.)

4. Preparing yourself. Take stock of your background, experience, and skills. Assess what you can do to prepare these for presentation. (See Chapters 9 and 10, especially the VWP guide.)

---

5. **Preparing and executing a job-search plan.** Most important for executing your search, make sure you match your talents, skills, and experience to job-market need and the potential employer. (See Chapters 8 and 9, especially the PEG matching Guide.)

6. **Marketing and selling yourself to the job market and potential employer.** Contact potential employers, job leads, and target companies. Develop job opportunities using known and unknown (to be developed) sources and contacts. Work all useful and effective avenues to potential employers. (See Chapters 4 through 12, using all effective sources and the TNT guide.)

7. **Gaining employer interest.** Complete initial contacts and introductions by telephone, resumé, cover letter and interviews. (See Chapters 4 and 9; make sure to use the 99-Minute Formula, VWP guide and, if necessary, the TART guide.)

8. **Completing the employer selection process.** Interviewing; work pending interest; negotiate and close the offer; or develop other opportunities. (See Chapters 7, 10, 11 and 12.)

9. **Starting the new job on the right foot.** The end of the job search is a new beginning.

Since careers and jobs are no longer lifetime commitments, your job talents are now governed as much by you as by your employer. In past years, improvement in an employee's job talents were often encouraged and pushed by employers. They were most often the motivating force. **Today, each individual needs to take charge of his or her own career growth and skills progression to meet both immediate employer and future job market needs.**

After learning what the job-search process entailed, Ted developed a job-search plan tailored to today's job market and similar to the following 11-step job-search plan. (Chapter numbers refer to *99 Minutes to Your Ideal Job.*)

Job-Search Plan

Completing the 11-Step Job-Search Plan Checklist[1]

**Check item
completed** ✔

__STEP 1. Get organized. A more difficult job market with on-going new developments means you'll need to not only *get* organized but *stay* organized. Pay attention to detail and to the new requirements and developments of employers. (See Chapters 3 and 5.)

__STEP 2. Identify your skills, experience, training and talent. Determine which of your skills are marketable, transferable, or crossfunctional. (See Chapter 6.)

__STEP 3. Determine your job and career interests, goals, and objectives. (See Chapter 6.)

__STEP 4. Become knowledgeable about the job market. Get in tune with employer needs and learn which job sources to utilize. (See Chapters 1 through 3, and 8.)

__STEP 5. Match your skills and experience to job market need. Fine-tune them as your job search progresses. (See Chapter 9.)

__STEP 6. Develop and execute your own tailored job-search and marketing plan to gain employer interest, interviews and offers.

   __ a. Use and improve traditional job-search techniques.
   __ b. Use nontraditional techniques and sources to the fullest extent. (See Chapter 9 on the TNT Guide.)
   __ c. Market and sell yourself. (See Chapters 9 and 10.)
   __ d. Gain employer interest; use the 99-Minute Formula. (See Chapters 4, 9 and 10.)
   __ e. Network to expand your sources. (See Chapters 7 and 8.)

---

[1]Ibid

__STEP 7. Assess and access the job market for both available jobs and potential opportunities. (See Chapter 8.)

___ a. Know openly available job opportunities.
___ b. Develop target companies.
___ c. Develop and find job opportunities.
___ d. Go after the behind-the-scenes and hidden job-market opportunities.
___ e. Work all sources and avenues.

__STEP 8. Be conversant with and knowledgeable about what is happening in:

___ a. your profession, career field and related fields.
___ b. business and the world today. (See Chapters 1 – 4.)

__STEP 9. Polish all your skills (communication, presentation, and job) to meet job-market need and stay ahead of your competition. Develop your presentation before you contact prospective employers and enhance it as your search proceeds. (See Chapters 4, 9, 10, and 13.) Include your

___ a. resumé, letters (cover, job search, follow-up).
___ b. introductory conversations (in-person, by phone).
___ c. interview (plan and practice) including the close and how to handle shortcomings.
___ d. closing and negotiating techniques.

__STEP 10. Evaluate and recalibrate your search activities for effectiveness as you proceed. Should problems develop

___ a. review your approach, techniques, and strategies.
___ b. work the turnaround guide (TART) if necessary. (See Chapters 9 and 14.)

__STEP 11. Continually use the new job-search guides, the 99-Minute Formula, VWP, PEG matching, TNT, and TART. (See Chapters 4 and 9.)

Setting Schedules and Making Plans

After reviewing the job-search process and completing a job-search plan, Ted developed a schedule to use in his job search. (See Appendix 1 in this workbook for forms to help you do this.) **Ted's overall scheduling scheme included daily and weekly activity lists, and a master work sheet for monitoring his progress.**

You can type your own calendar or schedule format if you wish, or add it to a regular calendar. Be sure to include all four activity categories:

1. Action items (calls, letters, work to do, etc.)
2. Research, source, networking contacts, etc.
3. Interviews and results
4. Follow up

To help in summarizing and keeping track of the multiple job-search activities required in a job search, see the Master Organizer Overview Works Sheet shown in Appendix 1, Exhibit 1.I. If available, you may find it helpful to use a computer with calendar/schedule software involving automatic follow up.

The search plan, schedule and calendar Ted established involved for the most part, working nontraditional job-search techniques. These techniques focused on using informational and inquiry calls, assertively networking with a systematic networking plan, and aggressively working a focused target-company list involving considerable direct employer contact. He also worked the job-placement industry for information and leads beside seeking available opportunities.

Developing a List of Target Companies to Contact

Ted's substantial research and sourcing of potential companies utilized many sources such as those outlined in chapters 3 and 8 of *99 Minutes*. He also used various directories and other sources that provide more detailed company information. Some of these are given in the Job-Source Information List in Appendix 6. Using all of these sources, he developed numerous potential employers and a target list of companies to pursue. You can use these information resources to develop a target list of your own.

Ted utilized work sheets (examples are provided in Appendix 1) to build his research, sourcing, and contact data, and diligently worked the networking and company-contact sources he developed. From this, he developed a list of target companies to contact. (See the shortened list that follows as a sample). You need to be certain all pertinent data is shown: full address, phone numbers, contact person, and brief notes on each company.

Three target companies are shown here so you can see the specific data to use in contacts with each company. Ted included additional companies in his list, all being either directly in or related to his areas of industry, background, and experience. You should list as much pertinent information as you can use, including the name of the individual hiring manager or person you want to contact. Use brief personal notes for background data and/or information you will want to use in establishing rapport with the interviewer and various company personnel.

Working All Effective Job Opportunity Sources

Ted was very successful in working his networking and direct employer contacts from the Target-Company List he developed by using telephone inquiry/information calls. He also pursued additional sources that provided opportunities and leads.

There are many additional effective sources available to work in developing job opportunities. Appendix 6 provides a lengthy list of job source information and directories. In addition, the insights provided from the Surveys*[1] in *99 Minutes to Your Ideal Job* (Chapter 3), provide excellent up-to-date data on the most effective sources used by survey respondents. Chapter 8 in *99 Minutes* provides a lengthy list of job sources opportunities both traditional and nontraditional. Chapter 9 provides effective methods of marketing and selling yourself to a variety of sources and avenues. In Chapter 7 (Clues to How Employers Recruit and Select New Hires) you will find a lengthy list of the Recruitment Sources Employers*[2] Use to Find New Hires. Also, you will find a reminder of job sources available provided on the last page of Appendix 6 (Job Source Information List) at the end of the workbook.

---

*[1] Thomas Mangum Company, *Job Hunter's Questionnaire for Executive, Management, Professional, and Technical Personnel*, 1993, 1994; Thomas Mangum Company, Job Hunter's Questionnaire for Hiring Managers, 1994.

*[1] & *[2] The Employment Management Association (EMA) and Thomas Mangum Company, (TMI). *Employment Market Survey: Employer Assessment of Current/Future Employment Market for Executive, Middle Management and Professional Staff*, joint project, 1993, 1994.

Sample: Target List Of Companies*

Company/Address Notes	Contact Name	Title	Phone/Rating/ Job Potential
1) EPA DEFENSE CORP. 342 Johnson Isle Lansdale, PA 12345	Herb Hoover James Adams	President VP Mkting	505/555-2233 A-rate/good potential
NOTES: Lead/Tim White. Same market as my background, appears nonaggressive competitor, lots of recent change, new VP. What's inter'l impact?	Herb has no inter'l experience		My exp is solid fit, may have apparent contracts need
2) IAS SYSTEMS 100 Deer Run Utica, NY 11107	John Monroe Lead/Ron Brown	President	209/555-1234 c-rate/good potential
NOTES: Lead/Paul Crist, Related market, Hear they want to enter market my background fits with inter'l push	John near retire- ment & may need backup. Div. may quietly be seeking replacement		Exp good fit to new mkt need and replacement possibility
3) PICO SIGNAL C & C DIV Tustin, Fl 13233 NOTES: Leads industry All markets, Hear they want to expand inter'l & seek more overseas markets	Ted Roosevelt E.D. Adams Previous Inter'l Mkt Mgr was promoted	Div Pres VP Mkting	208/555-3482 Rate high/good potential Restructure creates oppty

*All names and addresses are fictitious.

2

Gaining Employer Interest: How to Make Contact, Build Relationships and Interview Successfully

Finding a Job Opportunity Through Target Companies, Inquiry/Information Calls and Networking

Ted executed his job-search plan by pursuing a number of companies he felt would be especially suitable given his skills, experience and training. Ted worked his Target-Company List by making telephone inquiry/information calls and networking calls. Working systematically, he used information on his target list, a telephone/networking work sheet and a telephone call checklist (examples shown in Appendix l, Exhibits 1.F and 1.G). Ted's target list of companies included companies that especially suited his marketing and managerial skills that he believed would be very responsive to his international experience. In less than a dozen phone calls, Ted's target-company efforts yielded several opportunities. Other opportunities unveiled in Ted's calls provided interesting insights into behind-the-scenes job activity.

A Behind-The-Scenes Job Opportunity

Eureka! During one of his inquiry calls, Ted learned of a position possibility. His contact told him, however, that the job was still being discussed. It did not yet formally exist. **Ted had discovered a behind-the-scenes opportunity at stage two of the Employer Job-Opening and Recruitment Process. (This process is described in Chapter 8 of *99 Minutes*.) He knew of the job before it existed!** Ultimately, the position developed in the hidden-job market (also described in Chapter 8), and at that point Ted formally introduced his interest and capabilities, again, through an inquiry call.

During his call, Ted asked for a description of the position. A sample memo description is shown in Figure 2.1 with some modification for company confidentiality. Note that it is brief and lacks full detail, particularly the qualifications requirements.

Figure 2.1 **A brief position description obtained with an inquiry call through the "behind-the-scenes" job market.**

MEMO

JOB DESCRIPTION (JOB CODE 29)
Job Title: Director Electronic Business Development Systems Division

DEPARTMENT HEAD: **SALARY:**   **DATE:**
Johnson, E.   **Range $80-100/Bonus**   **1/5/94**

Purpose of Job
    -Under minimal supervision, establishes effective business contacts with customers for purpose of promoting and selling present and potential electronic products.

Primary Duties/Responsibilities
    -Directs marketing/sales activities of electronic products to agencies, private firms doing government business, and worldwide commercial aircraft business.

    -Directs development of short- and long-range objectives and recommends goals to higher management. Maintains key marketing/sales contacts with domestic and international, civilian and military personnel.

    -Assists in the formulation of advertising campaigns and approves publicity releases and promotional activities.

    -Advises management on status or action required in connection with existing and potential sales programs. Provides the company with information concerning government activities and competition which may affect company business. Performs other duties as assigned.

Matching Qualifications to Employer Need

The brief job description Ted received is all some companies have to work with as they begin their screening. In some cases the qualifications are more fully developed as the interview/selection process proceeds. In cases where the information is brief, it is not always reasonable to expect an employer to provide much detail in an introductory interest call. Still some probing to gain information may be helpful. In this case, the job-qualifications data was not developed enough for the employer to be able to elaborate with much additional detail. Without the qualifications requirements provided in the brief job description, Ted realized the initial job description was inadequate for matching his skill and experience to the employer's need.

While continuing his job search in other areas, Ted waited for a comprehensive qualifications profile to be developed for the Electronic Business Development Director's job. In a follow-up call made later, he learned that a comprehensive job-description and qualification profile had become available, and he requested a copy to review before responding with a cover letter and resumé. A sample of the detailed job-qualifications profile appears in Figure 2.2 with some modification for brevity and confidentiality. **Note the some *twenty* qualification requirements now listed (numbers identify each) in the detailed qualifications profile.** The initial brief description listed only eight. In most professional job-description/qualification profiles you will find a minimum of five to seven primary or key qualification requirement that allow for little variation. That is, a lower level of skill or experience that generally is not acceptable. Be sure to ask, as Ted did, what key qualifications the employer is striving to fill for the position.

Ted responded with high interest when he received the detailed job-qualifications description. It listed areas of experience desired by the company that fit his background very well and helped tremendously in framing his cover letter and resumé, and in later discussions and communications. The detailed description indicated the need for experience in at least ten areas for which he was well qualified. In particular, his experience in the areas of specific marketing management, product market experience, strategic and tactical marketing plans experience, contracts management and international experience really created high employer interest. In contrast to other positions, descriptions and companies Ted evaluated, this particular opportunity looked promising and one worthwhile to pursue.

Figure 2.2   A more detailed position description. Note the 20 qualifications requirements now listed.

Memo

Job Title: *Director of Electronic Business Development*

COMPANY DESCRIPTION AND LOCATION
Small division of a major Fortune 500 corporation that is a manufacturer in the aerospace, electronics and defense industry. The division is located in an attractive West Coast metropolitan area, with easy access to excellent recreation areas, colleges and universities, and a wide variety of cultural activities.

EXPERIENCE: [1]Position requires an individual with a successful marketing/business development record of performance in the areas of [2]Aerospace/Electronics/Defense and/or Avionics Systems. Requires [3]experienced marketing/business development manager selling to major aerospace, commercial electronics and avionic customers, [4]including international markets. [5]Background should include 15 years experience in succeedingly more responsible marketing and business development-type functions, progressing to [6]major product, program or division level marketing/business development management responsibilities. [7]Minimum five years management experience required (i.e. product, program, unit, or division.) Must have been through a number of [8]successful major marketing activities (i.e. market development/strategy, planning, contracts management, marketing/sales customer development, directing/[9]executing plan to successful conclusion. Requires a [10]professional, [11]mature person with [12]good presentation skills who [13]relates well with all levels of company and customer personnel. Must be a [14]"take charge"-type individual who is [15]innovative yet direct and [16]concise in his style, seeking an environment [17]offering personal, job, company and market challenge, and growth.

RESPONSIBILITIES: Same as in Figure 2.1.

EDUCATION: [18]BS or BA required, MBA preferred.

ORGANIZATION LEVEL: [19]Reports to President.

COMPENSATION LEVEL: [20]Base $90-110,000 year, plus bonus.

Ted reviewed the more detailed qualifications profile and ascertained the key qualifications for the position. He then responded with a well-written resumé and cover letter tailored to the job requirements and qualifications (PEG matching, see Chapter 9 in *99 Minutes.)*

The more detailed description convinced Ted he was an excellent fit for the position and it helped him in formulating his cover letter/resumé presentation. A sample resumé and cover letter are shown in Figures 2.3 and 2.4.*[1]

In addition to Ted's resumé and cover letter, you will find more sample cover letters and resumés in Appendix 2 and 3. Also you will find important resumé recommendations (format, content, length, features that have positive and negative impact) are provided in the survey results presented in *99 Minutes* in Chapter 10 (Your Personal Employer Introduction—Resume Comments and Suggestions) and Chapter 3 (Job market Surveys: New Tips and Trends to Help Job Hunters—Resumé Comments).*[2]

---

*[1] In Figures 2.3-2.5 amd 3.1-3.3 certain data, names and addresses are changed to protect confidentiality of individuals and companies involved.

*[2] The Employment Management Association (EMA) and Thomas Mangum Company, (TMI). *Employment Market Survey; Employer Assessment of Current/Future Employment Market for Executive, Middle Management and Professional Staff,* joint project, 1993, 1994.

Figure 2.3 Sample Successful Cover Letter. (Additional examples are in Appendix 2.)

3498 Julia Ct.
Garland, TX 73849
214/555-5678

Mr. William Mangum
Thomas Mangum Co.
123 Diamond Lane, Suite 222
Anytown, NY 12345

Dear Mr. Mangum,

I would like to join your client's marketing team! Please consider me in your search for Marketing Manager – Electronic and Avionic Products. You will find my professional experience an excellent match for your requirements.

o   Marketing Manager-Airborne and Electronic Products for two nationally-known medium-size avionics companies.

o   10 years experience in the sales and marketing of C^3, EW, and avionics products in domestic and international markets.

o   Experience in developing and reviewing both strategic and tactical marketing plans that recognize opportunities. Can address obstacles while staying focused on results and profitability.

o   Practical experience in writing and negotiating agreements with international agents and resellers.

o   Hands-on experience in bid-no bid decision making, managing a B&P budget, RED team reviews, proposal management, and win/loss lessons learned.

Enclosed is a copy of my resumé for your review. I would very much like to schedule an interview where we can discuss my background and the contribution that can be made to your client. You can contact me at the above address, or, if you prefer, you can reach me at 214/555-5678.

Sincerely,

Ted J. Smith
Ted J. Smith

Figure 2.4 Sample Winning Resumé. (Additional examples are in Appendix 3.)

Ted J. Smith   3498 Julia Ct.
                                                         Garland, TX 73849
                                                         214/555-5678

SUMMARY: Extensive background in marketing, business development, project management and engineering with expertise in satellite systems, ground stations, electronics and airborne systems.

Education: MBA, MSEE, BSME degrees, University of Wisconsin
Special knowledge in:
  o Sales and marketing of C^3, EW, and avionics products in domestic and international market including contracts and strategic planning

  o International joint ventures and strategic alliances

  o Commercialization of defense products and technology

EXPERIENCE
Astro Corporation, Electronic Systems Division, Dallas, TX

Director, International Business Development Mar. '90 - Present
Initiated international marketing and business development efforts from ground zero for Astro Electronic Systems Division. (1992 sales: $250M)

Selected Accomplishments
  o Identified $200M business opportunities for 1991-1995.

  o Accepted a challenge to win $100M in new business.

  o Created strategic alliances with international partners.

General Aerospace Corp./Astro Division, Dallas, TX 1980-1990

Manager, International Marketing, Asia-Pacific Jan '88-Jan '90
Led marketing and new business development efforts for GA Astro in the Southeast Asia and the Pacific Rim region. Led capture team for the successful PSIDIT ($100M) and CHINA ASAT ($175M) campaign.

Marketing Manager/Technical   Jan. '80 - Jan. '88
Managed technical, financial and scheduling aspects of projects.

A Winning Interview: Preparation and Effective Presentation

A week later Ted received an interview request. **He recognized the importance placed on interviewing in today's job market and worked hard to gather data and prepare himself for the interview.** In doing so, he developed an interview-preparation format to be sure he covered all essential items.

The Interview-Preparation Checklist in Appendix 1, Exhibit l.H, provides a detailed sample list to follow. It includes:

● Information essentials (items to be informed about).

● Interview preparation requirements.

● Interview presentation guidelines.

● Interview follow-up steps.

In preparing for the interview, Ted made a couple of phone calls to glean additional information. He called the search consultant and the human resources manager of the company to confirm the details of his visit. Sample questions, similar to his questions, are listed in the "21 Questions to Ask" Checklist, which appears later in this section. Ted learned a great deal that helped him zero in on company needs and problems and also on what kind of individual they were seeking. In following his Interview-Preparation Checklist, Ted completed most of the essential tasks and gathered all the information an aware job hunter needs for a winning interview presentation.

Questions to Ask Employers

Use the following list of questions as a useful guide to help you learn about a job, the company, and where it is located. In a telephone call before your interview, you will not be able to cover all of these questions. Ted, using discretion, saved some of his questions for the interview. He was sensitive to the amount of time an employer will spend and the amount of information an employer will provide in a phone discussion prior to an interview. Ted did, however, gain as much information as possible without turning off the person he was calling.

Prior to the interview, you should be able to gain general information on the first four basic questions on the list. *(They are marked with an asterisk.)* Plan on covering the additional questions in the interview. In some phone calls, though, you may be able to cover certain aspects of questions 5 through 11 if you have established good rapport, or are dealing with a search company or senior executive.

Remember, one of the best ways to *eliminate* yourself from serious consideration is to neglect to ask the interviewer some intelligent questions. This means that before the interview you must prepare yourself both with knowledge of the company and with questions for the employer. A written list is helpful and certainly reviewing the "21 Questions to Ask" Checklist will help in your preparation. Such information is also essential for your own assessment of the opportunity and the company involved.

"21 Questions To Ask" Checklist

Check questions reviewed ✔   ✔ **Check questions completed**

__1. *What qualifications are required and what are the general job responsibilities? Ask if you may review a copy of the job description for the position involved. (This is often not provided before the interview, but should be if it is available.) Check to see if the description includes the qualifications for the position. Find out some of the *specifics* of both the qualifications desired and the duties and responsibilities involved.   _____

      Such questions should cover:
      __   Experience - areas and specific type required and/ or desired; the level required.
      __   Education/training - years of formal education required (college, high school, etc.); other degrees or credentials required or desired; special training other than formal education or degrees.
      __   Skills required for position.
      __   Special abilities or skills not included in position description.

__2. *In terms of the organization, where is the job located? What are the reporting relationships (the person that the job reports to and other key individuals to which the position relates)?   _____

__3. *What is the organizational structure? Ask if there is a nonconfidential chart to review. Many companies do not release organization charts. Some companies will release these without individual names and other confidential data, or they may provide one during the interview.   _____

__4. *What is the compensation for the position? (Base salary, bonuses, incentives, etc.)   _____

__5. What type of individual is desired? Include

any special traits and characteristics desired to fit
into the company's organization and culture.   _____

__6. Why is the position available? Inquire about the
history of the position, the individual now holding
the position, and who previously held it. Has the
position involved substantial turnover? Of those
who left, what were their pluses and minuses? How
well did they perform and was their performance up
to expectations or beyond? The answers can be an
excellent tip off to the next three questions.   _____

__7. What accomplishments are expected?

__8. What are the expectations for the position and of
the new person in the position?   _____

__9. Are there any problems to be aware of and what
problems would a new individual encounter in the job?_____

__10. How are individuals evaluated for this position
and how often?   _____

__11. When do review periods occur? Are they tied to perfor-
mance increases? Do they occur separately? When?   _____

__12. What is the future of the organization?   _____

__13. What is the performance level and reputation of the
department and division related to the position?   _____

__14. How does the department, section, and division
fit into the overall company hierarchy as to capability,
respect, political clout, and ranking?   _____

__15. What are the promotional opportunities? How does one
advance their career with the company and how does the
promotion procedure work (formally and informally)?

Additional Question to Ask

Many additional questions will come up as job interest develops. I have listed some that can be helpful as the interview and selection proceeds. It is often helpful to jot down a list of questions on note cards, which can be referred to immediately prior to the interview.

__16. Can you provide more information about the company's marketplace, its markets, customers, competitors, standing, and reputation? _____

__17. What is the financial condition/stability of the company? _____

__18. Are there any business conditions or reversals expected that would impact the viability of the position, the division, or business in the near future? _____

__19. What are the employee benefits and eligibility requirements for health care and life insurance? _____

__20. Is travel or potential relocation required? _____

__21. A parting question useful for some interview closings: After reviewing our discussion today, I may have an additional question. May I call you? When would be most appropriate? _____

Employer Questions You May Be Asked

Ninety-nine interview questions are listed in Appendix 4 of this work-book. Ted answered many of these along with similar questions and became confident that he and the company were a good match.

In preparing for an interview, review these questions carefully. You will probably be asked many of the same or similar questions. Develop your own answers to the questions posed. You may also find it helpful to work with an interview primer sheet which includes your question list for your first few interviews.

Other Ways to Gather Employer Information

Ted was primed with substantial information about the company and the job from his pre-interview phone calls and from various inquiries and research. Beyond the information compiled from the Target- Company list,data on the company can be obtained from:

o Company annual and quarterly reports
o 10-Q and 10-K reports
o Stock and financial reports

He also talked with others in the industry about the company's reputation, and particularly about their marketing organization and its reputation. If published reports are not available, ask what the company can provide. You may need to gather your own data from individuals who know the industry.

Ted pulled together the essential ingredients for a solid interview with his preparation and effective presentation. If you can be as knowledgeable about a company as Ted was about this potential employer, match your skills to the employer's need as effectively as he did, and provide the employer with applicable skills, experience, and interest in a positive manner as Ted did, you will likely be on your way to becoming a serious candidate or receiving a job offer.

Providing and Prepping Your References

During the interview Ted was advised of the company's serious interest and was asked to provide references. Since he was currently employed and wanted to protect the confidentiality of his job search, Ted provided references on all previous employers excluding his current employer. Immediately following the interview he called all his references and, where it was appropriate, prepped them. It was particularly important to tell them of the confidential nature of his search. To protect the confidentiality of his current position, Ted only provided references of individuals not currently employed with the company.

References are a vital factor in achieving success in the interview and selection process. You should extend tender care in maintaining relationships with your references and particularly in keeping in contact with them as the years progress. In Ted's case, over the years he had lost track of one reference who covered a vital link for a substantial period of time. Ted had found this individual had given a hurried, quick reference on one previous occasion when he had not been advised in advance to expect the call. The quick reference was abrupt and although it was not negative, it was not as positive as it could have been. From this, Ted learned to nurture his references.

An Effective Employer Follow-up Letter

After the interview Ted composed a follow-up letter tailored to relate his skills and experience to the most important aspects of the job (see sample letter provided in Figure 2.5).*[1] Note where he relates his experience with NATO and its southern European countries to the company's need for international experience.

Also note the usefulness of his contract experiences which applies to their new products requirements and how he highlights his planning experience to an overall company need. He also includes a positive summary showing the value he could add to the company and the unique match of his skills and experience (PEG Matching). In addition, he affirms his ability to handle the challenge and opportunity involved and indicates he is looking forward to the prospect of joining ZYA Corporation.

---

*[1] Ibid

Figure 2.5   Sample Follow-up Letter to Prospective Employer

Mr. William Jones
Vice President Marketing
ZYA Corporation
555 Johnson Street
Elvira, WA 23212

Dear Bill:

I would like to thank you for the extensive time spent last week during the interview for the Director of Business Development position for your Electronics Products area. The position sounds like an excellent opportunity, and I look forward to the prospects of joining ZYA Corporation.

I enjoyed our discussion with Fred Phillips concerning the International Marketing responsibilities. My experience in the European market, particularly with NATO and the southern countries, would be most beneficial for your market development plans. Certainly my recent contact experiences will be useful in building new market contacts in your new product area.

My training and extensive experience in strategic and long-range planning should be helpful in your overall company planning activities for your upcoming five-year planning session and particularly for the coming year. As you know from our discussion, I am also formally trained in contracts management and feel comfortable with the new responsibilities we discussed in this area.

I am very interested in the challenge and opportunity provided in the position. I feel fortunate that my experience, skill and training uniquely provide the qualifications you are seeking. After evaluating the additional material on your new product activities, I feel I could contribute significantly to your new plans and to the company's short- and long-range goals. Additionally, my family looks favorably on returning to the Seattle area.

Should you have any additional questions regarding the European activity, please feel free to call me. I look forward to hearing from you soon.

Sincerely,

Ted Smith
Ted Smith

3

Evaluating, Negotiating, and Closing the Job Offer

Job-Search Success: An Offer Letter

After Ted's list of references checked out well, he received a follow-up call from Bill Jones, the Vice President of Marketing, to confirm Ted's continuing interest and commitment to making a change as well as a major geographic relocation. After reconfirming Ted's serious interest, Bill Jones reviewed in much greater detail the confidential aspects of the company's marketing position and what it expected to achieve in the market place.

He also reviewed with Ted again the challenges of the position and the expectations involved. Ted suggested a further discussion with the President regarding the long-range goals of the company to reconfirm the company commitment to its growth activity from both the President and Vice President including budget commitment. Within the next few days several telephone conversations were completed with the President, including a conference call with John Larson and Bill Jones resulting in a strong mutual feeling they were on track as to short- and long-term interests, goals, strategic-plan implementation, mutual interest and general compatibility.

Several days later Ted received a call from the Company Search Consultant to discuss the job parameters, personal compatibility of all key parties involved, along with the general parameters of a potential offer. The following week he received a verbal offer from Bill Jones, at which time he requested a written offer to review as shown by the sample letter in Figure 3.1.

Figure 3.1 Sample Offer Letter

Mr. Ted Smith
2234 Zinc Street
Balamor, NJ 19867

Dear Ted:

I am pleased to offer you the position of Director of Business Development for ZYA Corporation. In this position you will be responsible for all company marketing activities in the Electronic Product areas worldwide.

Your compensation package will be as follows:

Monthly salary of $8,700.00 per month
Bonus plan as outlined in Enclosure "A" including a minimum bonus guarantee of $15,000.00
Car allowance of $600.00 per month
Company paid (term) life insurance of $250,000.00
Company-paid medical insurance (80/20 indemnity), see enclosure "B" for details of plan including Dental plan
Vacation of three weeks per year, administered in accordance with ZYA personnel policies
401K plan
Relocation expenses per Enclosure "C"

All other benefits in concurrence with ZYA standard benefit policies, see enclosure "D."

I, together with John Larson and our Board, look forward to your favorable decision to join ZYA and to the substantial contribution we feel you can make to the organization. In addition, many of those you have met during your introduction and interviewing have indicated a strong hope that you will be the individual to lead ZYA Electronic Products Marketing activities.

Sincerely,

William Jones
William Jones
Vice President Marketing

Evaluating a Job Offer

A lengthy list of some 56 potential job-offer items appears as Appendix 5 at the end of this workbook. The short list here categorizes the items by key areas. In reviewing both lists you will see the extent of the items that can be involved in an offer, and why it is important to get the basics in writing.

Job-Offer Items Category List

1. Compensation
2. Transportation
3. Expense reimbursements
4. Credit cards
5. Communications
   (Field/home equipment, etc.)
6. Special allowances
7. Relocation costs
8. Travel cost
9. Benefits
10. Miscellaneous

In the long list you will find many of the more important items that job offers include. Keep in mind that an offer letter may not include all of the categories shown or many of the items mentioned in the longer list. However, an offer should include the basics of compensation (salary, bonus and/or incentives), title, name of your reporting manager, and department. A description of job duties and responsibilities is most often provided separately and should be requested if not provided earlier. Other items include relocation reimbursement and payment, a copy of the benefits package, special employment terms (i.e., severance pay if applicable, employment contract, and so on). Be sure you obtain all the basic information.

17 Questions to Help You Evaluate a Job Offer

When Ted received his offer he asked himself the following questions and so should anyone completing the same process.

**Check items
completed.** ✔

___1. Does the job meet my goals and objectives and are my objectives realistic?

___2. Is the offer clear and well-defined? Does it include the key areas of importance? What items are not included?

___3. What are the positives and negatives of the position? Develop a profit and loss grid on the position and list any questionable items to clear up.
Positive_____/ Negative_____/ Questionable_____

___4. Why should I accept the offer? (What do I like about the offer, position, and company?)

___5. Should I reject the offer? (What do I dislike about the offer, position, and company?)

___6. What will the job and the company do for me over the
___a) Short haul (1 to 2 years)?
___b) Long haul (3 to 5 years)?
___c) Does it help me to achieve my career goals?

___7. What is my motivation for accepting this offer? Is it valid?

___8. What is the viability and strength of the company? Is it profitable? If not, how extensive are its losses?

___9. What are the promotion opportunities?

___10. How do I really feel about the job, company, work environment, company culture, and the way employees are treated?

___11. Where am I in my job-search process, particularly in relation to other company interests, offer possibilities, or offers?

___12. Should the offer be accepted as is, negotiated, delayed or rejected?

___13. Should the offer be accepted for any or all of the following reasons: no other opportunities, unemployed, out of necessity, better opportunity, better job, more responsibility and challenge?

___15. Is the job a worthwhile short-term interim or stop-gap opportunity?

___16. Does the job offer new training/skill development?

___17. How well do I fit in with the prospective company? Consider the company's history, reputation, culture, and their goals and objectives (both for the company and the position involved).

Negotiating the Offer

After receiving the offer, Ted decided he should do more extensive homework on it. Since the new position involved a major geographic relocation, he was particularly interested in the relocation allowance and expenses. In addition, he wanted to gather data on what other companies' bonus plans were offering.

After doing his research and answering the preceding "17 Questions," Ted determined he wanted to negotiate the offer in several areas. He called William Jones, who signed the offer letter, to talk over the issues in detail. Ted emphasized his interest and concern in regard to several items of the offer. Following the discussion, he drafted a letter of response covering the points discussed in the telephone conversation. His letter suggesting revisions is shown as sample letter Figure 3.2. Note how Ted cites his strengths as a foundation for the offer revision. Also note the personal nature of the letter, and the praise he offers to all the key parties involved. His questions are straightforward, to the point, and relate to immediate items of interest to all. The tone of the letter is upbeat and positive in attempting to work toward a negotiated win/win result.

When you decide you want to negotiate an offer, you need to be prepared. You must gather your facts and information. Use the offer-items list in this workbook to help you gain needed information relevant to the items you want to negotiate. Preparation is essential for effective negotiations. In today's job market, you should avoid "winging" any negotiating effort. You must do appropriate homework and consider the other party's position. Successful negotiating works best when both parties come away from the effort feeling that they have succeeded in their efforts and objectives.

Consider your position and needs carefully as you work the following:

1. Define the parameters you want to negotiate
    a. What are the items/issues involved?
    b. Determine what you will accept.
    c Where will you give?
    d. Define your objectives.
    e. What are your needs?

2. Be patient and prioritize the items.

3. Gather your facts and data.

4. Determine the attitude/climate for negotiation.

5. Develop a win/win attitude and positive strategy.

Figure 3.2 Sample Successful Offer-Negotiation Letter.

Mr. William Jones
Vice President Marketing
ZYA Corporation
555 Johnson Street
Elvira, WA 23212

Dear Bill:

I enjoyed chatting with you last week and am sorry we could not arrange to meet in New York over the weekend. My schedule involved a company seminar the day you were passing through.

I just received your offer to join ZYA Corporation on Thursday and wanted to respond to you, as you asked, by the weekend. I sincerely believe I can make a major contribution to ZYA's business base in the Electronics Product areas. I feel particularly confident of meeting your goals for the new European products in the next eighteen months.

I like the ZYA organization, John Larson's participative management style and the technical, planning, management strength and enthusiasm you provide to the company.

Your offer is well presented, however, the proposed compensation does not represent much incentive for a change, particularly in light of the substantial relocation costs involved. I do not know your salary range for this position and the next-step position. Such information would be helpful. I would like to suggest we discuss adjusting the starting salary and/or the bonus base, recognizing my ability to jump start your European business base reaching projected goals twelve to eighteen months earlier than anticipated.

Participation in your Executive Incentive program is certainly a positive, and I like the way the program is structured. I would like to receive information on all levels of participation to evaluate your proposed 15% participation. I would also like to receive information on how the individual incentive percentage is calculated. Is the relocation package flexible and are there any provisions for spousal job relocation assistance?

Bill, we should continue discussions on the offer as we are close to establishing what I feel is a solid long-term working relationship to the benefit of all concerned. I am enthusiastic about your new products and the thought of joining the ZYA management team.

Sincerely,

Ted Smith
Ted Smith

The Amended Employer Offer Letter

Following receipt of Ted's letter about revising the offer, the company spent several days evaluating his suggestions. As a result, Ted received an amended verbal offer. Several days later he received an amended offer letter. The company revised its offer, as shown by the sample letter in figure 3.3.

Figure 3.3 Sample Amended Job-Offer Letter.

Mr. Ted Smith
2234 Zinc Street
Balamor, NJ 19867

Dear Ted:

Following our discussion last week and your letter, we are pleased to adjust your offer to cover the particular areas of concern you mentioned and to assist in your relocation efforts.

Monthly salary of $9,370.00 per month

The relocation allowance will be raised by $10,000.00 and the per diem will be extended to 60 days.

Spousal job assistance of $10,000.00 as a result of your spouse's unique job activity.

All other conditions of the offer letter of February 14 will remain the same. The physical exam we discussed can be taken in your area, and Jean Jackson of our Human Resources Organization will be in contact with you to arrange that next week.

Ted, we look forward to your favorable response. Should you have any additional questions regarding the benefits package and relocation assistance, please feel free to call Frank Jones, our Human Resources Director.

Sincerely,

William Jones
William Jones
Vice President Marketing

4

Starting Your Job Right: 26 Suggestions

A new job leads to new opportunities and challenges. To insure that you take maximum advantage of your new ideal job opportunity, I have included the following suggestions for getting started on the right foot.

Check item completed: ✔

___1.   Remember to thank those who helped you.

___2.   Maintain your contacts with your network on a semiactive basis and be prepared to reactivate it on short notice.

___3.   Use the homework and research you completed on the company. Enlarge on it to get to know the company, its culture, people, and ways of doing business.

___4.   Assess the capabilities of the organization and its relative strengths and weaknesses. Include those with whom you relate throughout the company and especially those individuals in your department. Ascertain what the relative rating of your department is in relationship to other departments (i.e., which departments sit where from top to bottom on the management totem pole)?

___5. Identify how things *are* done (basic operations) in your new company and how things *get* done (decision process).

___6. Develop a positive relationship with co-workers and peers. Establish several close relationships with peers and or managers who can assist you in ongoing relationships, people, project, organization, and company evaluations.

___7. Develop a mentor.

___8. Develop growth goals tailored to the organization with assistance from your superiors and the Human Resources organization (where helpful).

___9. Learn of the performance levels, goals, and objectives expected of you, your department, and the company for the coming year.

___10. Ascertain the company's performance review policies and procedures. Confirm what you were advised when hired as to when your performance reviews will occur (normally in six months or one year) and ask whether they relate to salary increases at the time of the review. If not, when do salary reviews occur (e.g., annually or within 60 days)?

___11. Be committed to add value by performing to your best capabilities in both what you can do (basic skills) and will do (motivation, enthusiasm).

___12. Consult with your superiors about what it is they want to achieve in their goals and objectives in the coming year. Clarify what role you are expected to perform in your position as to their expectations. This is most important because responsibilities and expectations can be, and often are, different. Ascertain what part you can play in those plans and work toward those objectives. Apply your strengths where they will be most helpful.

___13. Maintain a written log of your important activities and contributions. Highlight your accomplishments and the problems you helped solve.

___14. Develop and build an effective network of successful co-workers, particularly of co-workers who are contributors to the company's improvement, growth, and success. Avoid being associated with doomsayers and negative individuals who create more problems than they solve. You know the type—those who continually complain but have no suggestions and no willingness to expend their energy working toward solutions.

___15. Keep informed about what's going on; be involved in company activities—social, managerial, and recreational, etc.

___16. Be aware of the company's organizational power structure and how it works formally and informally. Observe the political nature of the players in the organization and the company's internal politics.

___17. Learn about opportunities for growth within the company and how internal promotions and transfers occur that can be beneficial to you.

___18. Be tuned in to the total organization as much as possible. Be aware of what's happening in other departmental areas, particularly those with which you interrelate and which impact your job function. By staying abreast of company happenings and activities you will become aware of problems and challenges you can participate in solving. This will add value to your contribution and enhance your opportunity for growth. You will also learn of opportunities which may interest you, that are in the development stage and before they reach the active recruitment stage.

___19. Be prepared to learn new skills, assume new duties and responsibilities, and reach out beyond your normal range of responsibilities, skills, and capabilities. Be positive in assuming new responsibilities. Be flexible and willing to develop cross-functional skills.

___20. Seek as much training and education as you possibly can, taking advantage of as much company training as possible.

___21. Ask your immediate superior and/or hiring manager as to what basis they will principally evaluate your performance over the coming year. Make notes of those items and be willing to seek guidance on any areas where improvements would be helpful.

___22 Create a win/win environment. Encourage open and straight-forward communications and show a willingness to listen and learn. Discuss work issues with your superior as the year progresses. This will help attain peak performance and reduce or eliminate major deficiencies, which could come as a surprise, and could hinder performance and promotional opportunities.

___24. Periodically (quarterly or semiannually) evaluate and assess your job performance on your own, separate from your superiors. This will help insure that you are prepared for your boss's performance review.

___25. Be aware of potential areas of danger that could affect you such as reorganizations, plant closing or moves, layoffs, downsizing, early retirements, etc. All of these are very common today.

___26. In today's competitive business world, remember employers are conducting probationary performance reviews of new employees in shorter intervals than in past years. Some 22% of employers questioned in an American Management Association report[1] said that in the last two years they had fired a professional or manager after less than three months. Be prepared to prove your value and establish a reputation as a performer early within your first year of employment.

---

[1]"Many New Executives Are Being Discharged With Stunning Speed." Wall Street Journal, March 4th, 1994.

Appendix 1

Sample Organizational Tools

Sample Organizational Tools

The tools in this appendix will help you plan your time and track your information. The schedules list steps to take. Additional work sheets will get you organized — providing contact, job source, target company, networking/telephone and interview tools including a master organizer to help you keep track of your work and its results by the four following categories.

1. Action items (calls, letters, work to do, etc.)
2. Research, sources, contacts
3. Interviews and results
4. Follow up

In developing your own job search schedule and campaign, keep in mind that each individual has his or her own style and work format. What is comfortable for one job hunter many feel awkward to you. Make adjustments accordingly. The following forms suggest a format to use that includes the basic and important items stressed in *99 Minutes To Your Ideal Job.*

In developing your own job search plan and in executing your campaign, you may find you want to vary the following suggested work schedule based on need, your current work schedule, or time availability. **Find what works best for you, remembering to include the basic elements outlined here.** If you are unemployed, you will find it beneficial to work the schedule on a full-time basis. For an employed individual, the schedule can vary considerably depending upon time available, the nature of your current work environment, and your sense of urgency and need about finding a new job.

Exhibit 1.A Initial Job -Search Activity—
Week 1 Schedule and Checklist:

Check item ✔
completed.

__ **DAY 1**

__ Make the decision to find a new job—the ideal job.

__ Get organized.

  _1. Begin gathering your working tools and materials.

  _2. Learn about the job-search process and what is required to develop your own job-search plan.

__ Begin job market evaluation (These are daily and ongoing.)

  _1. Learn what jobs are available.

  _2. Learn where potential opportunities can be developed.

  _3. Utilize information gained from your job market evaluation gained on an ongoing daily basis. Use the work sheets in Appendix 1 and the Contacts Work Sheet (Exhibit 1.C) to assist in evaluating and gathering job market information. Also use the Job-Source Information List in Appendix 6.

__ **DAY 2**

__ Develop your own job-search plan (see Workbook Part 1).

__ Begin self-assessment process.

  _1. Work the self-assessment checklist questionnaire (in Part 1 of this workbook) and answer as many questions as you can. Keep the list available, review and update it on a weekly basis.

  _2. Continue your self-assessment and work the personal

assessment process in Chapter 6 of *99 Minutes* to determine your total skills, capability, interests, goals, traits, etc.

____ Finish getting organized and gathering work materials.

____ Begin developing your initial resumé rough draft. Allow yourself sufficient time to get a clear understanding of your skills and experience from your self-assessment and job-market evaluation so you can focus on developing an effective, well presented quick-glance resumé. A one-page resumé is recommended. Two pages is the maximum length.

____ **DAY 3**

____ Begin networking. Formulate an extensive networking list using the worksheet provided in Appendix 1, Exhibit 1.G.

____ Complete self-assessment process to establish your total capabilities (skills, traits, etc.) and your interest inventory. This will help you focus on what you have to offer and what you want to do regarding your objectives and goals.

____ Use the information from your self-assessment in your job-search plan and campaign for networking, employer contacts, etc.

____ Use the self-assessment in your job-market evaluation.

____ Relate and match yourself to available jobs and potential employer opportunities by using the self-assessment data.

____ Review your resumé draft using self-assessment insights.

____ Finalize your job-search plan and complete as many plan activities as possible. Monitor your plan on a weekly basis.

____ **DAY 4**

____ Summarize your job-market knowledge gained to date.

Remember your job-market evaluation is an ongoing process and will continue throughout your job search. As you learn more about the job market and potential employers you will adjust and fine-tune your job search efforts. It is essential that you continually assess and evaluate the market so you can relate and match your skills and interest to job-market and employer needs.

____ Begin your company research and sourcing. Search for companies and positions suitable to your skills, interests, objectives, and goals.

    __1. Develop a list of target companies to contact using a format similar to Ted's Target List of Companies or the sample form in this appendix (Exhibit 1.E).

____ Begin to finalize your initial resumé utilizing the recommen-dations in Chapters 4 and 9 in *99 Minutes*. Be prepared to revise it as your search progresses.

    __1. Review what you have learned about the job market, available jobs, potential job opportunities and your self-assessment. Apply this to your resumé.

    __2. Review your resumé with qualified professionals in the job-placement industry to assure it meets today's market needs. Also utilize employer feedback as your job search progresses.

__DAY 5

____ Develop a telephone presentation to use with employers and individuals with whom you will be networking or using as a third party for introductions.

    __ 1. Work up a written outline of your telephone presenta-tion in a prompter-type format that is easy to follow. It should include a verbal three-minute resumé. Use the Telephone Call Prompter Form in Exhibit 1.F as a guide.

____ Complete several practice introductions. Select several companies that are not primary in your areas of job interest and call to practice your telephone presentation.

____ Begin drafting your initial cover letter for the written presen-tation you will use with resumés presented to employers and individuals with whom you network. Your cover letter will vary depending upon the company, the skills and experience required, etc. It needs to be tailored to the company and individual written to and will vary based on the knowledge you have gained about the company.

____ Set up a work schedule by week (preferably by day) for the next several weeks of your job-search campaign. Focus on:

__ 1. Working all effective job-market sources.

__ 2. Developing as many job opportunities as possible that are applicable and related.

__ 3. Contacting all available job opportunities that are applicable and related.

__ 4. Completing your initial target-company list with sufficient companies and names to start and complete the second week of your job-search schedule.

Exhibit 1.B   Weekly Job-Search Schedule and Checklist

The weekly job-search schedule can be used week by week as your search progresses. It includes activities for a full week's effort. It can be completed weekly by many individuals committing full time to their job-search efforts. If you are employed, try to work the items into your schedule as best you can, remembering to work a few items each day so you do not lose your job-search momentum. In all cases it is important to keep your momentum going!

The checklist can be used for each succeeding week of your job search by noting at the top the number of the week you are working and the week's date. To track your progress, record for each checklist item the cumulative count of the tasks completed over the current week and each succeeding week of your job search. For instance, 30/120 for item 1 below indicates you completed 30 phone calls in the current week and 120 total calls since your search began.

Check item completed. ✔	Week_/total_ Date____

__1. Telephone 50 contacts (10 per day) to find job opportunities and get referrals using networking and employer introductory and inquiry calls.   __/__

__2. Utilize all sources (traditional and nontraditional) that include openly available jobs as well as behind-the-scenes and hidden job-market opportunities.   __/__

  __a. Be assertive in developing opportunities from from the total spectrum of the job market.   __/__

  __b. Continue gathering job-market information and employer research and sourcing, particularily for applicable target-company contacts and introductions.   __/__

  __c. Add 10 companies to your target list. Call and send letters/resumés where appropiate. Always direct the letter to an individual; use a name or personal referral, or indicate a contact source or research source. Express interest & match qualifications to company need.   __/__

    __ d. Follow up with calls and schedule appoint-   __/__
ments or obtain a future interest possibility or
other lead possibilities.

__3. Work placement industry organizations (search,   __/__
outplacement, contingency, assistance groups, etc.)
suitable to your job interest, skills, goals and
objectives.

    __a. Work temporary and interim employment-   __/__
placement companies.

    __b. Work-placement industry companies (executive   __/__
search, agencies, etc.) for leads and potential
opportunities aside from specific job openings.

__4. Work potential part-time, temporary, and consulting   __/__
opportunities.

__5. Respond to all openly available job opportunities,   __/__
advertisements, postings, word-of-mouth, tips and
so on related to your interest and objectives. Have
friends and business associates keep you posted on
opportunities that develop from various areas such
as company bulletin boards and newspaper job
listings, industry and professional listings, etc.

__6. Read and keep up-to-date on professional, industry,   __/__
market, and trade journals related to your job skills
and interests. Keep notes and gather contact information on authors, editors and the names of individuals
you can use for contacts and leads. Stay current on
general business, technical and product/marketing
articles related to companies in your areas of
interest.

__7. Do lots of elbow-rubbing (meeting potential   __/__
professional leads and employers). Attend meetings
and social functions of associations related to
your area of skills and interest. Develop contacts
and acquaintances.

__8. Contact college placement offices, department heads,   __/__
professors in your areas of interest as to opportunities,

leads and potential interim, temporary, part-time or consulting opportunities.

__9. Establish a follow-up procedure with your job   __/__
contacts, leads, employers and potential
employers and follow up regularly. Send thank-
you notes emphasizing your interest and, where
applicable, your qualifications.

Exhibit 1.C Contact Work Sheet: All Sources

   To simplify gathering your total contacts, use a single contacts list. You will be surprised how quickly this list can build. I suggest categorizing and identifying your contacts by an abbreviation rather than using several lists. List all sources of potential job opportunities by identifying the source such as: friends(F), acquaintances(A), professional associates(PA), professional organizations members(PO), business contacts(B), media(M), college(C), classmate(CM), advertising(AD), publications(PU), customer/clients/competitor(CCC), associations(AS), and so on. Create other categories if you need them. Be sure to identify all networking contacts with a large **N** designation. From your research and sourcing list designate these by using a large **RS** to highlight your target company leads.

Referral Name and Source	Category	Company Referred	Category
1. Al Tays / FEI*	PO	Allison Co*	**N**
2. Ed Riley / GE	CCC	Carter Co	**N**
3. Bill Culey / Allied	AS	CPI Systers	**N**
4. Tim Wheeler	AD	AO Mfg Co	WS Journal
5. Bob White	PU Moody's	Ester Fan Corp	**RS**
6. Ted Jakes	PU Dunns	Cable Stran	**RS**
7. Paul Obey	AD	Carson Online	NY Times
8.			
9.			
10.			
11.			
12.			

*Sample Fictitious Names and Contact Sources

Exhibit 1.D   Individual Job Source Work Sheet

Some job hunters find it helpful to work with individual lists and, for ease of use, combine them later. If you prefer to work with several lists instead of one, you can start with the following:

o Publication list—Listing all that relate to your interest
o Networking list (friends, associates, business contacts)
o Association list
o Target company list
o Media and advertisements list

Example: Individual Publication Work Sheet

List all publications that will provide you leads related to your job, career field, industry/business and interests. Your contacts with your industry/business associates, customers, competitors, and vendors can provide the names of pertinent publications. You can also gather material from the library, industry/business associations and publications seen in the various offices of the your sources.

Publication*	Area/Specialty	Job related
1. WS Journal	Financial Analysis	Morgan Guarantee
2. FEI Journal	Planning & Strategy	Cann Investment
3. Investors Daily	Trends	Security Holdings
4.		
5.		
6.		
7.		

*Sample Publication Source Data

Exhibit 1.E   Target Company Work Sheet

COMPANY, ADDRESS AND NOTES ON PRODUCTS/SERVICES AND COMPETITORS	CONTACT(S)	TITLE(S)	PHONE, RATING, JOB POTENTIAL

Sample Company #1

| XYT Products 121 Larson St Ely, New York 11224 | Al Smith | Pres | 555/333-3333 |
| | Clare Wong secretary | | My experience highly suitable, could be their Ops Mgr and pres backup |

Notes

| Consumer plastics. Competitors competed with daily/Same market customers, company less aggressive marketeer and poor reputation. Smith has no backup & weak Ops Manager. | Know Jim Jones | QC Mgr | |
| | Ted Crisp | CEO | Worthwhile potential |

Company #2

ADDRESS AND NOTES, ETC.	CONTACT(S)	TITLE(S)	PHONE, RATING, JOB POTENTIAL
_____	_____	_____	_____
_____	_____	_____	_____
_____	_____	_____	_____
_____	_____	_____	_____
Notes _____	_____	_____	_____
_____	_____	_____	_____
_____	_____	_____	_____

Exhibit 1.F   Telephone Call Prompt Checklists

One of the most important steps in your job-search campaign is effectively introducing yourself to employers and contacts that may lead to the opportunities they offer. Preparation is most helpful for many individuals. It does not require an extensive effort. Only a few solid preparation steps are required. Some experienced job hunters say they find it helpful to develop their own telephone call prompter for their initial calling efforts. You may find this tool can help you focus on the important items to discuss in the short time period available for a telephone presentation. Follow the basic steps here and you will find your calls become easier to make, helping you to quickly convince an employer you can add value to their organization.

**Check item
completed.** ✔

___1.   Plan your presentation.

___2.   Gather some advance information on the individual you are calling and on the company. You can use this in your conversation.

___3.   Work out the format and items you want to present.

___4.   Outline and note which items have the highest priority. Allow some flexibility to accommodate the responses and questions of the person you talk to.

___5.   When you call, identify clearly who you are.

___6.   Always use a **name-referral** source, if possible.

___7.   Use a **subject** source, particularly if name referral is not available.

___8.   Use a **source of interest to the recipient,** if possible.

___9.   Be confident. Provide a brief, clear and concise statement of why you are calling.

___10. If you sense the recipient is rushed, has a meeting going, or prefers not to continue the conversation for some reason, ask: Is this a convenient time to talk or would you prefer

I call back at a more convenient time?

___11. Build rapport. Quickly sense, from homework, company data and from discussion, several items of interest to recipient.

___12. Draw out the recipient's interest in utilizing high-quality talent in their organization.

___13. In providing your **presentation**, focus it on

    ___ a.   their interest.
    ___ b.   a referral source.
    ___ c.   your **mini-resumé** presentation.
    ___ d.   a statement on the **value you can add** to the organization.

___ 14. Maintain a **two-way conversation interspersed with a few questions** during your comments.

___ 15. Be brief, positive, and to the point on your skills and experience.

___ 16. Suggest a short meeting. State that you look forward to meeting to get acquainted, to discuss **some common areas** (developed from conversation and your homework), and to discuss what you can offer that would **benefit the company.**

___ 17. If at first your conversation does not succeed, be pleasant. Say you will call back at a more convenient time (ask when) or later when a need exists. Indicate you look forward to talking on the date selected, or "again soon" if no date is set.

___ 18. If action is left open-ended inquire as to suggestions and opportunities elsewhere or other individuals to contact.

___ 19. Be persistent. Take busy and rushed conversations as a sign of busy times, not a brush-off. Such conversations and initial rejections often can be turned around to eventual job opportunities or leads.

___ 20. Remember these basic mechanics of an effective phone call:

    ___ a.   Be pleasant.
    ___ b.   Smile as you talk.

___ c. Listen carefully.

___ d. Visualize a friendly conversation you are prepared and confident to handle.

___ e. Conduct the conversation at a moderate pace, varied in tone and expressing a positive and enthusiastic attitude.

___ f. Include questions and seek suggestions.

___ g. Be professional and express some knowledge of the relevant field, industry and marketplace.

___ h. Include an appointment suggestion or request.

___ i. When the conversation is completed, the employer

     ___ knows who you are.

     ___ has some understanding of what you can do.

     ___ recognizes that you are knowledgeable about their business and market.

     ___ knows that you feel you can be of value to the organization.

     ___ is aware you feel you are qualified and fit the needs for an available or potential position (if that is the case).

     ___ knows that you want to meet.

     ___ is encouraged to respond to your request for a meeting or a future meeting with a time set for the meeting or follow up.

     ___ is asked to provide leads and opportunities when no specific opportunity or meeting results.

___ 21. Be prepared for a 5- to 10-minute presentation. It should include a quick and succinct verbal resumé presentation of important experience/background/education/training if necessary or requested. Relate background as much as possible to company's business, activities, market and specific job if available. Be flexible and prepared for a shorter conversation as well as the opportunity for a lengthier discussion. See Chapter 4, the 99-Minute Formula (Personal Sales Opener); Chapter 9, Marketing and Selling Yourself (Your Presentation: Verbal, Written and Personal); and Chapter 10, Your Personal Employer Introduction (Your Verbal Introduction).

Using the Telephone and Networking Worksheet

In today's lean and difficult job market, surveys show that the majority of job opportunities are developed or occur through telephone, networking and personal contacts. While this may surprise some job hunters, it will not come as a surprise for those who have read *99 Minutes* and the survey data provided in chapter 4. Conversations with successful job hunters also show that telephone and networking contacts are most important in executing a successful job search with companies that either have job opportunities available *or may have potential job possibilities.*

Exhibit 1.G that follows, provides a 2-page telephone and networking work sheet, that combines much of the important information to gather and use in individual company contacts. The worksheet prompts the gathering of essential data to use for an introduction such as basic company information, contact person and title, source and contact name, key company notes, results, etc. The source and action columns require key information/action for effective communication and presentation. The footnote sections provide some 24 source and action items to assist, speed and record your company contacts process. Don't be hesitant to add additional information you feel may be helpful.

In utilizing the Telephone Call Prompt Checklist (previous Exhibit 1.F), with the Telephone and Networking Worksheet, you have available at your finger tips the essential tools with which to work. Remember, in a tight job market where employers, hiring managers, human resource personnel and networking contacts are overworked and overloaded, a second opportunity may not necessarily come around again. **Some individuals and employers tell us that networking is so extensively used today, that they are cautious how they spend their networking and contact time. In today's very busy and time pressured business world, this is an important reason for improving your networking contact effectiveness and *using all effective job sources.*** Make sure all your contacts, telephone and networking efforts are organized and planned. Be prepared to be as effective as possible by using all the tools, information and skills you have available and can develop.

Exhibit 1.G   Telephone and Networking Worksheet Organizer

SOURCE	ACTIVITY STATUS AND ACTION REQUIRED**			
Company/person, Address/phone	Date	Person/title	Source of contact*	Source name
Sample				
XYZ Products 221 Jay Street Phoenix, AZ 85001 206/333-9999		Ted Jones VP Mkting Wm. Ties QC Mgr.	(F) Friend* (M)Media	Wm. Ties Ted Ray Prof. at Yale, Dr. Wan

Company/person #1

_____	__	____	____	____
_____	__	____	____	____
_____	__	____	____	____
_____	__	____	____	____
_____	__	____	____	____
_____	__	____	____	____

Company/person #2

_____	__	____	____	____
_____	__	____	____	____
_____	__	____	____	____
_____	__	____	____	____
_____	__	____	____	____
_____	__	____	____	____

Company/person #3 (etc.)

* Indicate source of contacts

Acquaintance (A)	Customer/Client/	Publications (PU)
Advertising (AD)	Competitor (CCC)	Networking (N)
Association (AS)	Classmate (CM)	Research/Sourcing (RS)
Business Contact (B)	Media (M)	Vendor/Supplier (V)
College (C)	Professional Assoc. (PA)	

Exhibit 1.G (cont.)

Key notes, comments	Action required,** date	Interviews, meetings/ date	Follow-up, date	RESULTS
Sample				
Mention Ray's comments on Q & Mat'l. problems/my solutions & Professor Wang referral	Call Jones hiring mgr., has solid reputation Call Ties** before Jones		Thank Wang	This one looks promising. Send references & meet Jones' boss

Company/person #1

____	____	____	____	____
____	____	____	____	____
____	____	____	____	____
____	____	____	____	____
____	____	____	____	____
____	____	____	____	____

Company/person #2

____	____	____	____	____
____	____	____	____	____
____	____	____	____	____
____	____	____	____	____
____	____	____	____	____
____	____	____	____	____

Company/person #3 (etc.)

**Action required
For each individual and company indicate as shown by the following examples the contact action required:

Cold call	Network call	Hiring manager associate
Lead contact	3rd party	Senior staff
HR department	Senior mgmt.	Follow-up call
Placement industry	Corp. mgmt	Send letter, resumé,
Other _____	Hiring manager	Follow-up letter

Exhibit 1.H Interview Preparation Checklist

The time spent in an interview, often an hour or so, is pivotal to achieving success in your job search. The 99 Minute Formula described in Chapter 4 of *99 Minutes To Your Ideal Job* focuses on essential elements in your interview presentation. (Also see Chapters 9 and the three interviewing chapters—10, 11, and 12.) During the interview the employer will evaluate your positive and negative factors in relation to the position you seek. **Preparation is essential for a winning presentation.**

Check here. ✔
___ 1. Be informed
    ___   as much as possible about the job.
    ___   about the company.
    ___   about the market the company is involved in.
    ___   about the job market.
    ___   about the business areas related to your job
           interest and the employer you are interviewing.

___ 2. Be prepared.
    ___   Be aware of potential employer questions and
           be prepared with your responses. (See in this workbook:
           99 Employer Questions You May Be Asked.)

    ___   Know what questions you should ask and know
           which ones you want answered specifically. (See in
           this workbook: 21 Questions to Ask Employers Checklist.)

    ___   Gather company data
        ___   on market and product information.
        ___   on key executives.
        ___   on pertinent financials, stock, and
             related company business, professional
             and community involvement.
        ___   on competitors.

    ___   Prepare your own personal presentation. Be sure you
           know yourself. (See Chapter 6.) Use this checklist!

    ___   Dress the appropriate style for the employer (usually
           conservative, expecially if you are unsure). Check your
           grooming from head to toe: shoes shined, pressed cloth-
           ing, color-coordinated clothing, and so on.

     __   Be aware of appropriate demeanor.

     __   Gather all data you can about the employer's job description and qualifications required.

     __   Have appropriate samples of your work available to present if necessary.

     __   Have your presentation organized. (See Chapters 4 and 9.)

     __   Have your resumé available and appropriately prepared for the position and the company. (PEG Matching, etc.)

     __   Practice being a good listener and observer.

     __   Be aware of illegal interviewing questions.

__3.   Practice and visualize your presentation. Remember, practice will help greatly in an effective presentation. It will arm you with a knowledge of the essentials to cover. Most important, it builds confidence.

__4.   Know the basics for your interview presentation.

     __   Be positive and enthusiastic. Utilize the 99-Minute Formula and the VWP Guide. Always maintain a positive attitude.

     __   Be on time for the interview. Allow sufficient time so you are not late. If early, review your presentation briefly before the interview. (Visualize Success!)

     __   Be pleasant, friendly and smile.

     __   Begin the introduction with a firm handshake. Be aware of your nonverbal forms of communication. (See Chapter 10 in *99 Minutes.*)

     __   Present relevant data on your skills, qualifications and experience. (See Chapter 9 of *99 Minutes* on the PEG Matching Guide.)

___ Recognize that nervousness and anxiety are normal.

___ Know and present all appropriate skills, experience, interests and accomplishments.

___ Structure your questions and answers specifically for the position and the company involved.

___ Request to see a copy of the job description and obtain a copy if available (assuming it was not obtained in your pre-interview data gathering).

___ Respond to questions in a clear and succinct manner.

___ Be concise. Avoid lengthy descriptions involving work assignments, activities, accomplishments, and other matters, unless you are specifically asked for more detail.

___ In the course of the interview, show some of your knowledge gained about the company and its marketplace. Use what you know about company individuals and the company to your advantage in building rapport.

___ Do not hesitate to ask appropriate questions.

___ Be aware of interview turnoffs such as being overbearing or aggressive; being a know-it-all and/or being conceited or presenting an impression of superiority; being passive and showing indifference; being evasive and making excuses; placing too much emphasis on yourself as the sole reason for prior company and department success; chewing gum, poor hygiene, having bad breath, avoiding eye contact with the interviewer, being fidgity; discussing personal problems and making negative comments about prior jobs, employers and superiors.

___ Summarize your presentation and highlight your strengths relevant to the requirements of the position and company need.

— Close by indicating your interest, inquiring as to the
next step (if not indicated), requesting written company information (such as an annual report), and
requesting business cards from appropriate individuals
met (hiring manager, human resources, etc.).

— Use discretion regarding compensation. Generally,
let the company initiate salary and related discussions. When appropriate, inquire about performance-
evaluation methods and any special compensation
plans that may apply (sales and/or incentive bonus,
etc.).

___ 5. Follow-up the interview.

— As soon as possible following the interview write a
summary of it. Highlight key items for follow up.
Include items you may need to use in subsequent
interviews and additional closing techniques to
apply. Note the positives and negatives of the interview, and also the pros and cons regarding the job
and the company. List what interests you and what
turns you off.

— Send a follow-up thank you letter. Where appropriate,
highlight one or more of your relevant strengths. Include positive comments on some individuals met and
the company.

— If mutual interests exists, gather additional necessary
data. When serious employer interest develops, do
your homework for evaluating, negotiating, and closing the job offer. (See Chapter 13 in *99 Minutes,* and the
56 Potential Job-Offer Items Work Sheet in Appendix 5.)

1.I   Master Organizer Overview Work Sheet

SEARCH ACTIVITY   Week #__ (_/_/_)

Start Date (_/_/_)   Week#1 (_/_/_)   Week#2 (_/_/_)   Week#3 (_/_/_)
Sample: (2/1/95)   (2/8/95)   (2/15/95)   (2/22/95)

Search
steps completed   _____   _____   _____

Job market info.
and research
completed   _____   _____   _____

All source
contacts &
leads developed   _____   _____   _____

Target companies
developed   _____   _____   _____

Calls and
networking
completed   _____   _____   _____
(all calls—cold, leads, network, company, placement firms, etc.)

Letter/Resumé
contacts/mail
completed   _____   _____   _____
(all—Sr. mgmt., hiring mgr., HR Dept., staff, corp. 3rd party, etc.)

Follow-up/calls
activity   _____   _____   _____
(all—network, 3rd party, company, placement firms, etc.)

Interviews   _____   _____   _____

Key comments   _____   _____   _____
and feedback   (use notepad for additional notes)

Evaluation/mid-course adjustments and corrections.
Changes to make? Yes_____No   Yes_____No   Yes_____No

Results   _____   _____   _____
   Contacts   _____   _____   _____
   Interviews   _____   _____   _____
   Offers   _____   _____   _____
   Acceptance   _____   _____   _____

Appendix 2

Cover Letters Samples

Cover Letter Reminder Notes

● Note in the Sample Letters section the following:

   • Letters are addressed to a specific individual.

   • Letters include a referral name source (name of company employee if possible) or a referral subject (specific position, need, possible need) and/or a topic of interest to person and/or company addressed.

   • Relevant experience cited, either as to position available, potential position available or value that may be added to the company by job applicant (not always required in networking letter).

   • Specific experience cited in position advertised letter with several or various areas of applicable experience cited for the position requirements.

   • Accomplishment listed briefly where applicable.

   • Buzz words included that relate to company business, needs, markets and activities.

   • Letters indicate action and results desired.

● Review *99 Minutes* for additional cover letter suggestions

   • Chapter 3   (Survey Results—Cover letters)

   • Chapter 4   (99-Minute Formula, 30 Seconds: the Magic Door Opener)

   • Chapter 9   (Cover Letters)

GENERAL LETTER SAMPLE

827 Trent Road
Spokane, WA 82792

Ms. Paula E. Thompson
Vice President, Programs
Zilo Aircraft
212 Airport Way
Burbank, CA 91504

Dear Ms. Thompson:

I would like to present my background for the position of Program Manager, a position for which I am well qualified. I am confident from my discussion with Ted White, your Operations Vice President that I can make a major contribution to Zilo's program management business functions.

I have an outstanding track record managing new and complex programs. Examples of my accomplishments include:

  o 90% on-time program completion.

  o 45% "follow-on program" development success.

  o 90% on-target budget completion.

  o New programs development in 1 out of 3 customer areas.

I believe I can make contributions to Zilo in your complex programs, both nationally and internationally. Additional background includes an M.S. in Program Management from USC Graduate School, plus a total of 20 years experience in Engineering, Marketing and Program Management.

Should your organization need an outstanding Program Manager who can make immediate contributions to your aircraft business and add profit to your bottom line, I can be reached at 206/555-4529 during the day and 206/555-9986 during evenings and weekends. I look forward to hearing from you.

Sincerely,

Robert Jones

Robert Jones
Enclosure

NETWORKING LETTER SAMPLE

135 Ardis Way
Chicago, IL 83694
312/555-1234

Mr. Ed Smith
Vice President of Engineering
Z Corporation
111 Edison Avenue
Libby, AZ 85232

Dear Mr. Smith:

Chris Johnson, a friend and former Division Manager from Taylor Johnson Industries, suggested I contact you. Chris was associated with Z Corporation many years ago and has been a customer of Z Corporation for several years.

While attending an Instrumentation Association meeting with Chris last week, I confidentially mentioned my interest to him in changing positions because of a need to relocate to the West Coast. Chris suggested that you are also very involved in industry activities and you might have some suggestions on job opportunities in the Southwest and California areas.

Since your firm is a leader in instrumentation, I felt you might also be aware of opportunities suitable for my experience in the medical instruments field, particularly sensor instruments. I recently read about some of your company's new product activities in galvanic instruments and was intrigued by your new approaches.

I will be in Tucson the week of February 24 and would welcome the opportunity to meet for coffee or lunch at your convenience. I look forward to such a meeting and, in the meantime, to hearing from you regarding any industry suggestions you might have.

Sincerely,

Bill Sample

Bill Sample

Enclosure

POTENTIAL JOB AVAILABLE LETTER SAMPLE
Matching Experience To Potential Need

361 DuBarry Street
Weatherstone, PA 19463

Mr. Hall Jackson, President
XYZ Corporation
800 Star Street
Pasadena, CA 91101

Dear Mr. Jackson:

During a recent telephone discussion with your Vice President of Operations, Earl Wheeler, I was advised that you are considering installation of a MRPII system at XYZ Corporation and will be in the market for someone who can provide strong leadership to your materials management organization. I am well qualified in materials management and experienced in the implementation of the MRPII system.

Experience and training include a Master of Science degree and over fifteen years experience in the field of procurement and materials management. One of the MRPII systems recently installed received industry recognition. I have also provided leadership in the development of MRPII systems application in other divisions and have been credited with improving the operation's performance for which the company has realized substantial gain. I am confident I can make similar contributions to XYZ Corporation and would like to meet with you to discuss the challenges and opportunities involved.

I will call you within the coming week to determine your interest and look forward to the possibility of meeting with you.

Sincerely,

Claudine Sample
Claudine Sample

CS/ar
Enclosure

ADVERTISED POSITION LETTER SAMPLE
Matching Experience to Specific Position Available

451 Allison Dr.
Los Cruces, NM 86067
502/555-2256

John Jones, President
Astor Corporation
1700 Castle Street
Phoenix, AZ 85613

Dear Mr. Jones:

The enclosed resumé is in response to your ad for a Director of Marketing.
I believe you will find my fifteen years peripheral products experience
combined with my graphics and multimedia background meet three key areas
of your job requirements. My experience covers:

- Serving as President of National Media Graphics (NMG).

- Identifying growth-market opportunities and delivering successful
  products nationally and internationally.

- Developing new distribution channels and marketing programs.

- Establishing solid credibility with customers, dealers and others in the industry.

I have a BS and MBA, and I have held positions such as:

- Marketing Manager of a $100 million computer graphics peripherals business.

- Vice President Marketing and Sales of a multimedia high-technology,
  technological-breakthrough company.

- Vice President Marketing for a $70 million computer graphics and
  software company.

Please review my background relative to your needs. I look forward to the
opportunity to meet with you.

Sincerely,
Mike Adams
Mike Adams

Appendix 3

Resumé Samples

Resumé Reminder Notes

● A note regarding the use of resumés and those shown in this section. Experience and survey results show that in a lean and difficult job market for job hunters, the unsolicited resumé, particularly one sent without a cover letter and not addressed to a specific individual, receives minimal response. Often the best that happens with an unsolicited resumé without a cover letter, is that it is held in the company's retrieval system. There are always exceptions that occur such as a **well-written resumé,** received at the right time and place, that fits an immediate need. Pure luck or a combination of both may be sufficient as long as the resumé is **well written and laid out.** Survey results show, and employers strongly recommend, the need for cover letters.

● Employers and executive search and placement firms have used various types of resumé retrieval systems (manual, electro-optical and computer) for many years. More companies today utilize such systems effectively, particularly computer systems. Recent studies show a relatively high acceptance of automated applicant retrieval and tracking systems by employers, executive search and placement firms, and job data banks. When job hunters ascertain no further current interest exists or no current opportunities are available, they should not hesitate to inquire and encourage companies to keep their resumé in their retrieval system.

● The overall use of electronics in the process of employers communicating job opening in the job market to job hunters and visa versa, in candidate recruiting, screening and in resumé processing continues to increase as equipment and software costs come down and technology improves. On-line computer services, Internet, E Mail, bulletin boards, and computer data bank usage is growing rapidly. Another example is the electronic scanning of resumés with computer retrieval systems. While scanning is not extensive, its use is also increasing. A listing of Job Data Banks, Computer Database, and On-line Services are provided in Appendix 6. Several books published in 1994, providing updated information in these areas, are also listed in Appendix 6 (Electronic Source Information).

● Review *99 Minutes* for additional resumé suggestions.

- Chapter 3   (Survey Results)

- Chapter 4   (30 Seconds: The Magic Door Opener)

- Chapter 10   (Resumé Comments/Suggestions)

Robert Sample
20586 Peach Tree
Nashville, TN 40387   614/555-2345

Controller/Treasurer with substantial experience in building products and food containers. MBA and BS Physics (UCLA). Experienced in team management and TQM. Strong quantitative abilities at coordinating simultaneous tasks. Experienced in financial leadership: Accounting, Treasury, MIS, and Planning areas.

EXPERIENCE

James Products, Nashville, TN, Controller   1990 - 1994

Single-plant manufacturer of building products growing at 70% per year with 1993 sales at $15 million. Responsible for closings, letters of credit, MIS, and Credit Department.

o   Installed PC network, and implemented training for all office personnel, increasing ability to handle rapidly growing workload.

o   Upgraded inventory tracking system, decreased bookkeeping errors, avoided missed sales by eliminating inaccurate reports.

o   Upgraded and computerized the Credit Department providing up-to-the-minute customer reports and financial status.

Solomon Corp., Nashville, TN, Assistant Treasurer   1977 - 1990

$200 million food container and paper products manufacturer with 15 manufacturing locations. Managed Treasury, Financial Analysis, Credit and Cash. Responsible for banking relationships, loan covenants, short-term and capital investments, supplier and customer contracts, credit limits, letters of credit and UCC filings.

o   Created and managed treasury/financial analysis department to establish control over cash flow and reduce working capital by $10 million.

o   Created a standard cost system to project profitability and cash requirements. Implemented computer modeling.

o   Analyzed and presented financial evaluations for expansion, resulting in acquisitions totaling $55 million in annual revenue.

Professional affiliations: FEI, NAA, EIA, SEC, AMA. Detailed affiliation, training and activities list available.

FRANK SAMPLE

251 East Drive   **Santee, CA 94588**   **919/555-1234**

EXPERIENCE OVERVIEW - MBA and BS degree, Oregon State

Background involves a unique combination of experience in marketing communications and building sales. Positions have included comprehensive marketing management responsibilities as Vice President of a major advertising agency and President of a marketing firm assisting major technology companies such as Moon, Microsoft and Zenith in setting up stronger sales channels.

The last two years have served as V.P. Marketing at Moon Technology (9/93 to date). During this period, company grew from the #3 terminals manufacturer in the world to #1.

Over career have developed successful strategic marketing programs for some 25 technology and non-technology companies.

PRIOR EXPERIENCE

White Technology   San Ramon, California   10/87-9/93

White is the leader in terminal manufacturing and an open-system provider of client-server computer products with $200 million in annual sales.

Vice President of Marketing: Expanded direct-MAR channel 40% and lowered sales support costs by over 35% during the same period. Set up telemarketing department to qualify the customer base and targeted prospects. This department today supports MAR and distributor sales, including 15 different categories of MARs and distributors worldwide; also generates 20% of domestic sales.

Recently completed the new sales strategy for distributing White products and this has been put into effect including a major revision for Japan, Singapore, Hong Kong and mainland China.

The Systems Group   Austin, Texas   7/78-10/87

Nationally recognized technology marketing firm assisting major high-tech companies to set up stronger sales organizations. 80% in the MAR/SI environment.

President: Co-founded firm with clients including major corporations such as Apple, ROM, Northrop, Lexis, Next, and AMC.

Assisted client in landing the EPA/General Suppliers engineering software business with new support concept. Client won the business over ATT and ATT later bought client. Recommended restructuring and downsizing from 700 resellers to less than 200 and expanded the new 150 "targeted" customer base.

CAROLYN SAMPLE

555 Newton Street   718-555-6746
Highland, NY 11356   Fax 555-5732

SUMMARY: MA and BA degree (Harvard) with 15 years administrative experience as Director, Manager and Assistant. Special strengths involve customer relations and managing complex multimedia, publication and high-technology administrative organizations.

EXPERIENCE:
Director of Administration WTA Corp., Pala, NY   1989 - present

Managed administration and supported the president in starting up and managing a rapidly growing new line of business.

> Reorganized operations except research. Exercised high level of judgment/discretion with minimum staff/supervision.

> Performed all customer-relations functions and human-resource support functions.

> Organized and arranged the logistics of business activities for both domestic and international business operations.

> Proficient with IBM and Macintosh computers using Excel, Multimate, Microsoft, and Lotus.

Manager of Administration App Tech Corp., Caster, NY   1982 -1989

Responsible for all administrative management and customer relations activities of a $190 million corporation with nine offices worldwide.

> Reorganized administrative and customer-relations function and reduced staff 25%.

> Led management team responsible for increased performance and major savings resulting in 29% profit improvement.

> Managed total quality function on interim basis resulting in dramatic reduction of returns and hiring of quality manager.

Administrative Assistant Trist Company, Erie, PA   1979-1982

Supported General Manager in $150 million spin-off sold to competitor. Responsible for all administrative management functions. Developed customer relations and service function with 50% reduction of field offices and 29% improvement in customer services.

Detailed affiliations (ASA, FEI, AMA, etc.) and activities list available.

JOHN E. SMITH
Post Office Box 98376
Atlanta, GA 30359
(404) 555-8311

Over 25 years of progressive and challenging experience in behind-the-camera work for local and network news services. Expert with a wide variety of state-of-the-art broadcast equipment and have covered wars, revolutions, celebrations, hurricanes, political campaigns and celebrity interviews around the world, on call constantly and traveling across the country and the world with little or no advance notice.

Experience

FREE LANCE   Mid 1993 to Present

Various jobs with local stations and networks in news broadcasting including consulting, remotes and editing

CBS NEWS   Atlanta, GA   1967 to 1993

Technical Supervisor, Film Camera Operator
Videotape Editor and Camera Operator

• Handled daily remotes during Desert Storm from Egypt, Jordan, The United Arab Emirates, Israel and Saudi Arabia with anchor Dan Rather in a different country daily. Personally ran computer communications, editing and teleprompter.
• Involved in every space mission since Apollo 9, first as cameraman then supervisor.
• Covered political campaigns of Hubert Humphrey, John Lindsey, Jimmy Carter, Ronald Reagan and Bill Clinton among others. Following Clinton in 1992, relocating daily. Set up remote broadcast sites, downloaded scripts from computer, printed and entered them on electronic teleprompter for evening news.
• Worked hurricane coverages. Team won national Emmy for Hugo coverage.
• Covered Civil Rights demonstrations and disturbances in the South during the 70's decade.
• Assigned to special events coverage worldwide involving Sadat assassination, Lt. Calley trial, the Royal Wedding, Kissinger Shuttle Peace Talks in the Middle East, etc.
• Functioned as Film Cameraman, Videotape Cameraman, Computer Specialist, Videotape Editor, Satellite Uplink Operator (fixed and portable), Maintenance Engineer, Microwave Installer, Crew Coordinator, Technical Director, Computerized Portable Teleprompter Operator and Local Purchasing Manager.

Professional Development

George Washington University—Satellite Transmissions
Cleveland Institute of Electronics—First Class License
University of Oklahoma—News Photography
Sony Broadcast Training

Computer literate (MS-DOS and Windows platform). Lotus, WordPerfect 5.1, 5.2 & 6.0, D-base, Pro-com Plus, Basys and Newstar.

Appendix 4

99 Employer Questions You May Be Asked: Checklist

99 Employer Questions You May Be Asked: Checklist

Review each question and **check the column on the left upon completion.** Space is provided for brief notes. You may find it useful to keep all of your answers to interview questions in a separate notepad. As your job search progresses you may find it helpful to note new questions that occur and to review the more pertinent questions in your early interviews.

Employer/Former Employer Questions

✓

__1.   Why are you changing jobs? Why did you leave your last employer, former employers?

__2.   What happened on your last job? Were you laid off, terminated, or did you quit voluntarily?

__3.   Why were you laid off, terminated, or fired?

__4.   How do you feel about your employer or former employer? How do you feel about being laid off or terminated?

__5.   Why have you changed jobs so often?

__6.   What salary/compensation were you earning?

__7.   What do you like most and least about your job? Your prior jobs?

__8.   What did you like most and least about the company and prior companies?

_9.   What do you like most and least about your supervisor?

_10.   What is your opinion about your company, your prior company?

_11.   How much did you interact with your supervisor's boss, and what did you think about your supervisor's boss?

__12.   You changed jobs a lot. Why? How long would you stay with our company?

__13.   What was your work schedule like? How many hours did you work?

_14.   Why did you work so much overtime?

_15.   How would you describe the management style of your present company and supervisor and of your prior company supervisor?

_16.   What will your supervisor say about you?

_17.   Tell me about your job. Describe it and your duties and responsibilities.

_18.   What were the major problems you encountered in your job/prior job and how did you handle them?

_19.   What are (were) your major accomplishments with your employer (former employer).

_20.   How did you help your company reduce costs?

_21.   In what way did you help your company build profits and sales?

_22.   What contributions did you make that improved quality and customer service?

Job/Management Performance Questions

__23. What kind of performance reviews did you receive? How often and how were you rated by your boss?

__24. How is/was your job performance measured? How do you measure the job performance of your subordinates?

__25. In which areas did your supervisor rate you high and low?

__26. What is your greatest strength? What weaknesses do you work most to improve?

__27. What do your superiors consider to be your major strengths and weaknesses? Do you agree?

__28. What have you accomplished in your present job? In your prior positions and jobs?

__29. How would you describe your management style? What type of manager are you?

__30. How do you motivate and encourage people?

__31. Do you prefer working through other managers? Are you a hands-on manager? Are you a leader?

__32. Describe a typical day's activity in your current or previous job.

__33. Do you feel that you are/were overworked?

__34. What are or have been the important problems you have had to deal with? What setbacks have occurred and what have been your real successes?

__35. What is the most difficult aspect of being a manager?

__36. How do you go about hiring people? How do you evaluate them?

__37. How do you reprimand individuals, and how do you handle terminations?

__38.   Describe some approaches you would use in persuading and encouraging others to work with you.

__39.   What do you do when you are not satisfied with the performance of subordinates?

__40.   How satisfied were you with your performance? What do you do when you are not pleased with your own performance?

__41.   Describe some specific activities, projects, and ideas you have developed on your own that have made some impact.

__42.   How did you go about accomplishing these activities, projects and ideas and what was their degree of success?

__43.   How have you helped improve your company's business and operations?

__44.   What commendations have you received, and what suggestions for improvements were made?

__45.   What is your definition of a successful employee/manager?

Questions about Relating with Others

__46. How well did you get along with your supervisor and his boss?

__47. How well did you get along with your peers and subordinates?

__48. How well do you think your supervisor got along with you?

__49. What were your relationships with others in your department and the company? With whom did you work most closely?

__50. With what other individuals, peers, and subordinates did you work closely or relate to? How did those relationships develop and what were the results?

__51. With whom did you work most effectively, least effectively, and why?

__52. With whom did you find it easiest to work, the most difficult to work, and why?

__53. Why were you not successful in the XYZ project after being successful in the ABC project? With what individuals did you work most successfully in both projects? With what individuals did you work less successfully and why?

Personal Preference Questions

__54. What are your career goals, work goals and personal goals and objectives?

__55. What do you like to do most and least?

__56. What type of company do you prefer to work for as to:
>   a. size (small, medium or large)
>   b. type (private, public, nonprofit)
>   c. management style (participative, authoritative)
>   d. structure (highly-organized, structured, unstructured, entrepreneurial)
>   e. market/product/service provided

__57. What are you looking for in a new job? Why are you interested in this job and what are your expectations?

__58. Why are you interested in our company?

__59. Why do you want a new career or different career direction?

__60. What additional responsibilities are you interested in and qualified to assume?

__61. What activities do you engage in to improve your job knowledge? How do you keep up-to-date in your field and in business? What do you read to keep up-to-date?

__62. Describe the type of people with whom you like to work.

__63. How would you describe your work ethic?

__64. What kind of work environment do you like or prefer?

__65. Do you like to work in a structured environment or an unstructured environment? A highly active, busy, moderately busy, even-paced or slower-tempo environment?

__66. Do you like to work under pressure: all of the time, part of the time, or not at all?

__67. What do you know about our company and industry?

__68. Are you able to relocate?

Key Employer Interest Questions

__69. What kind of contribution do you feel you could make to our company and how long do you estimate it would take?

__70. What is there about our company that interests you?

__71. How would you sell our product and company?

__72. Why should the company hire you?

__73. What other jobs are you considering?

__74. If you had your "druthers," what would you avoid in your next job?

__75. Describe your career, its progression, and what you have accomplished. What are your future plans?

__76. Is this an appropriate position for you? You appear over-qualified for the requirements of the position.

__77. Since your experience is light for the position, is there any significant aspect of your experience and skills that would offset this shortcoming?

__78. What salary/compensation are you looking for?

__79. Describe how you feel your experience and capabilities apply to the position available and the company?

__80. Is there anything you would like to add to our discussion at this time?

__81. What important elements are you looking for in your next job and in the job you are applying for? How is that different from your current or former job?

__82. What can you tell me about yourself? Describe yourself and your personality.

__83. Why should I hire you? Why should our company hire you?

__84. What are your major strengths and weaknesses?

__85. How do you handle criticism?

__86. Have you been involved in leaderhip positions outside of your employment (i.e., fraternal, alumni, or service organizations, Toastmasters, Junior Chamber, etc.), volunteering for charity, fundraising, self-improvement, political support or community betterment.

__87. Do you consider yourself a team player?

__88. Do you consider yourself a leader?

Schooling, Formal Education and Training Questions

__89. What is the extent of your formal education? What degrees and diplomas have you earned?

__90. What additional training and schooling have you had?

__91. Have you had any special training (i.e., management, professional, technical, trade, craft, etc.)?

__92. Why did you decide on your specific area/s (i.e., environmental sciences, engineering, business management, etc.)?

__93. Why did you choose to attend USA University rather than American College or Westminster University?

__94. What was your major and why?

__95. What kind of grade-point average did you have, overall and in your major? What were your best and poorest grades?

__96. What classes, subjects, and activities did you like the most and the least?

__97. How was your education financed (i.e., scholarship, self, family, joint, loan program, other)?

__98. What activities and school leadership responsibilities were you involved in?

__99. Why did you change colleges, majors, and/or have gaps in your education?

Appendix 5

56 Potential Job Offer Items Worksheet

56 Potential Job Offer Items Worksheet

Your offer comparison

Compensation

1. Salary _____

2. Bonus _____
    a. Eligibility factors and basis for determination
    _____
    _____ (circle one)
        b. Incentives   Yes / No
           Type and basis for determination
    _____
    _____

3. Stock options   Yes / No
        Type: matching( ) phantom( ) grant( ) other( )
    _____
    _____

4. Profit-sharing plan_____ Yes / No
    _____
    _____

5. When do performance reviews occur? 6mo( ) 1yr( )
    18mo( ) 24mo( ) open( )

        a. Are they tied to compensation increases?   Yes / No
    _____
        b. Or annual review?   Yes / No
    _____

6. Termination/severance pay   Yes / No

    _____

7. Other   Yes / No

    _____

Transportation

1. Auto allowance   Yes / No

    _____

2. Company car   Yes / No
    a. Lease   Yes / No
    b. Reimbursement   Yes / No
    c. Operating expense   Yes / No

    _____

3. Other   Yes / No

    _____

Expense Reimbursement

1. Transportation   Yes / No

    _____

2. Clubs and other memberships   Yes / No
    a. Clubs — country( ), health( ), social( ),
    b. Memberships — professional( ), trade( )

    _____

3. Other   Yes / No

    _____

4. Credit cards   Yes / No
    a. Telephone   _____   Yes / No
    b. Gasoline   _____   Yes / No
    c. Air travel   _____   Yes / No

    _____

5. Other   Yes / No

    _____

Communication (Field, in-home equipment, etc.)

1. Cellular phone   Yes / No
2. Beeper   Yes / No
3. Telephone   Yes / No
4. Office equipment   Yes / No
5. Fax   Yes / No
6. Network links   Yes / No
7. Computer   Yes / No
8. Other   Yes / No

Special allowances

1. Financial( ) and tax assistance( )   Yes / No
2. Estate planning   Yes / No
3. Legal, etc.   Yes / No
4. Other   Yes / No

Relocation

1. Moving expense (household goods relocation)   Yes / No

---

2. Relocation cost   Yes / No
       a. Total   Yes / No
       b. Partial   Yes / No
       c. Tax gross payment   Yes / No

3. Special offsetting upfront bonus   Yes / No

---

4. Company purchase of home   Yes / No

---

5. Real Estate transaction costs
       a. complete or   Yes / No
       b. partial real estate closing Yes / No

---

6. Mortgage points( ) fees( ) appraisal( )
    inspection( ) other( )   Yes / No

---

7. Legal expenses   Yes / No
    _____

8. Mortgage assistance   Yes / No
    _____

9. Automobile transport reimbursement   Yes / No
    _____

10. Special home care   Yes / No
    _____

11. Temporary living allowance   Yes / No
        a. Per diem   Yes / No
    _____

        b. Motel/hotel   Yes / No
    _____

12. Other   Yes / No
    _____

Travel cost

1. House-hunting trip cost   Yes / No
    _____

2. Home relocation/cost differential for higher
    cost of housing   Yes / No
    _____

3. Special relocation allowance payment to include
    all or part of the above   Yes / No
    _____

4. Travel expenses and per diem   Yes / No
    _____

5. Per diem payment for temporary housing   Yes / No
    _____

6. Other   Yes / No
    _____

Benefits

1. Vacation_____ # Days___
2. Holidays_____ # Days___
3. Health( ) and life insurance( ) _____ Yes / No
    a. Standard   Yes / No
    b. Extended   Yes / No
    c. Executive   Yes / No
    d. Disability   Yes / No
    e. Dental   Yes / No
    f. Visual   Yes / No
    g. Psychological   Yes / No
    h. Additional   Yes / No

    _____
    _____
    _____

4. Pension Plan   Yes / No

    _____

5. Continued salary benefit during illness/incapacity   Yes / No

    _____

6. Education benefits   Yes / No
    a. Education/training reimbursement   Yes / No

    _____

    b. Management/executive programs   Yes / No

    _____

    c. Graduate degree tuition fee program   Yes / No

    _____

7. Other   Yes / No

    _____

Miscellaneous

1. Termination agreement   Yes / No

    _____

2. Employment agreement   Yes / No

    _____

3. Outplacement   Yes / No

    _____

4. Other   Yes / No

    _____

Appendix 6

Job-Source Information List

Job-Source Information List

One of the best sources of job information is your local public library. University and college libraries are also great sources, if you have one nearby. Librarians, particularly research or reference librarians in larger libraries, are almost always very helpful. Many libraries have a business and directory section available for easy use. Some have database capabilities through their computers.

Some of the publishers of the directories below also publish additional directories and will provide a full listing upon request. Toll-free 800 telephone numbers are often provided.

Resources and Directories

Specific Directory (name, publisher and telephone)

America's Corporate Families
Dun & Bradstreet Information Services, 800/526-0651

Associations Yellow Book
Monitor Publishing Co., 212/627-4140

Chamber of Commerce Directories, (by individual city)
City Business Directories/Buyers Guides are
published independently or sponsored by
a specific city's chamber of commerce.

Business Organizations, Agencies and Publications Directory
Gale Research Inc., 800/277-GALE

Commerce Register's Directories of Manufacturers
Northeastern United States
Commerce Register Inc., 800/221-2172

Corporate Yellow Book
Monitor Publishing Co., 212/627-4140

Consultants and Consulting Organizations Directory
Gale Research Inc., 800/277-GALE

CorpTech Directory of Technology Companies
Corporate Technology Information Services, 800/333-8036

Directory of American Research and Technology
Reed Reference Publishing, 800/521-8110

Directory of American Firms Operating in Foreign Countries
Uniworld Business Publications, 212/697-4999

Directory of Corporation Affiliations
National Register Publishing Company, 800/521-8110

The Directory of Executive Recruiters
Kennedy Publications, 800/531-0007

Directory of Foreign Firms Operating in the U.S.
Uniworld Business Publications, 212/697-4999

Directory of Human Resource Executives
Hunt-Scanlon Publishing Co., 800/477-1199

Key European Executive Search Firms and Their U.S. Links
Kennedy Publications, 800/531-0007

Directory of Management Consultants
Kennedy Publications, 800/531-0007

The Directory of Outplacement Firms
Kennedy Publications, 800/531-0007

Directories In Print
Gale Research Inc., 800/277-GALE

Directory of Top Computer Executives
Applied Computer Research, 800/234-2227

Dunn's International Directories
Dun & Bradstreet Information Services, 800/526-0651

Dun's Business Rankings
Dun & Bradstreet Information Services, 800/526-0651

Dun's Directory of Service Companies
Dun & Bradstreet Information Services, 800/526-0651

Electronic Industry Manufacturing & Telephone Directory
Harris Publishing Company, 800/888-5900

Encyclopedia of Associations
Gale Research Inc., 800/277-GALE

Encyclopedia of Information Systems and Services
Gale Research Inc., 800/277-GALE

Federal Yellow Book
Monitor Publishing Co., 212/627-4140

Hoover's Handbook of American Business
The Reference Press, Inc., 800/486-8666

International Directory of Corporate Affiliations
National Register Publishing Company, 800/521-8110

Manufacturers' Directories (by state)
Manufacturers' News, 708/864-7000

Manufacturers/Business Directories (Western States)
Database Publishing Company, 800/888-8483

The Million Dollar Directory Top 50,000 Companies
Dun & Bradstreet Information Services, 800/526-0651

Million Dollar Directory Series
Dun & Bradstreet Information Services, 800/526-0651

Moody's Industrial Manual
Moody's Investors Service, Inc., 800/342-5647

Moody's International Manual
Moody's Investors Service, Inc., 800/342-5647

Moody's Municipal and Government Manual
Moody's Investors Service, Inc., 800/342-5647

National Directory of Nonprofit Organizations
The Taft Group, 800/877-TAFT

National Directory of Addresses and Telephone Numbers
Omnigraphics, Inc., 800/234-1340

National Trade and Professional Associations
Colombia Books, Inc., 202/898-0662

Polk City Directory
R.L. Polk & Company, 800/275-7655

Reference Book of Corporate Managements
Dun & Bradstreet Information Services, 800/526-0651

Research Centers Directory
Gale Research Inc., 800/277-GALE

Standard Directory of Advertisers
National Register Publishing Co., 800/521-8110

Standard Directory of Advertising Agencies
National Register Publishing Co., 800/521-8110

*Standard & Poor's Register
of Corporations, Directors and Executives*
Standard & Poor's, 800/221-5277

Telecommunications Directory
Gale Research Inc., 800/277-GALE

Thomas Register of American Manufacturers
Thomas Publishing Company, 212/695-0500

Value Line Investment Survey
Value Line Publishing, Inc., 800/833-0046

Ward's Business Directory of U.S. Private and Public Companies
Gale Research Inc., 800/277-GALE

World Aviation Directory & Buyer's Guide
McGraw-Hill, 800/257-9402

World Business Directory
Gale Research Inc., 800/277-GALE

Human Resources, Outplacement, and Placement Industry Sources

The Directory of Executive Recruiters (See Directory list)

Directory of Human Resource Executives (See Directory list)

The Directory of Outplacement Firms (See Directory list)

The Association of Executive Search Consultants (AESC)
Members only, Directory available for purchase, 212/949-9556

The Best Directory of Recruiters
Gove Publishers, 508/957-6600

Employment Management Association
Directory for members only

Executive Employment Guide
American Management Association, 212/903-7912

Hunt-Scanlon Job Seekers Guide to Executive Recruiters
Hunt-Scanlon Publishing Co., 800/477-1199

National Association of Personnel Services (NAPS)
Members only, Directory available for purchase, 703/684-0180

Society of Human Resources Management
Directory for members only

The International Association of Corporate and Professional
Recruiters (IACPR), Directory for members only

Job-Source Publications and Opportunity Listings

Career Opportunities (4 Newsletters)
CEO UPDATE, 202/408-7900

Dun's Employment Opportunities Directory
Dun & Bradstreet, 800/526-0651

Exec-U-Net newsletter job listings, 203/851-5180

Encyclopedia of Career and Vocational Guidance
J.G. Ferguson Publishing Company (4 volumes) • 312/580-5480

Job Hunters Source Book
Job Seekers Guide to Private and Public Companies
Gale Research Inc., 800/255-GALE

JobBank Series (i.e., Chicago, Seattle, New York, etc.)
Bob Adams, Inc., 800/872-5627

Job Seekers Source Book
Donald D. Walker, Valerie A. Shipe
Net-Research 708/739-0093

Job Market Directory
Job Hotlines USA
Career Communication Inc., 800/346-1848

NetShare newsletter job listings, 415/883-1700

National Business Employment Weekly
Wall Street Journal, 800/568-7625

Search Bulletin newsletter job listings, 703/759-4900

Job Opportunities (4 books), Peterson's Inc., 800/338-3282

Job Choices: 4 Volume Career Planning Job Search Reference College
graduate series. College Placement Council, Inc. 800/544-5272

Electronic Source Information

Computer Database and Online Services

Dun & Bradstreet Information
800/223-1026

Moody's Rating Delivery
212/553-7904

Disclosure Online
800/945-3647

Standard & Poor's Register
212/208-8429

Dialog
800/334-2564

Dow Jones News Retrieval
800/522-3567

Corporate Technology Database
800/333-8036

CompuServe Information
800/848-8990

Lexis/Nexis, 800/227-4908
(Includes New York Times
data link)

Prodigy, 800/Prodigy
(Includes Los Angeles Times
data link—800/792-Link X274

CareerMosaic Internet hookup (Access to certain company job opportunities and information via internet. Some college campus placement offices have internet links as well.) Type http: / /www.careermosaic.com.

Job Webb Internet Hook-up through World Wide Web via Mosaic and Netscape, etc. Type http://www.cpc.org
Available to all job seekers, College Placement Counsel, Inc.

Job Data Banks

Job Banks USA
800/296-1USA

Adnet Online
800/682-2901

CareerNet
800/392-7967

Publications Available

Electronic Job Search Revolution: Win with the New Technology That's Reshaping Today's Job Market

Electronic Resumé Revolution: Create a Winning Resumé for the New World of Job Seeking
Authors for both books: Joyce Lain Kennedy and Thomas J. Morrow
John Wiley & Sons Publisher, 1994

Job Seekers Guide to Online Resources
Kennedy Publications, 800/531-0007

Hook Up, Get Hired, The Internet Job Search Revolution
Joyce Lain Kennedy, John Wiley & Sons Publisher

Organizations Providing Call and Fax Responses

These organizations will send you articles, company information, financial data, etc. (Inquire about rates.)

Article Clearing House, 800/521-0600

Los Angeles Times, Times on Demand, 213/237-6999

Ask Dow Jones/Journal Finder, 800/759-2797
Wall Street Journal, Barron's and Dow Jones News Service

Associations

Encyclopedia Of Associations
See Directory list

National Trade and Professional Associations
See Directory list

The Encyclopedia and National Trade Associations Directories list thousands of associations with association data and contact information. Some associations provide members with help in their job search by providing various services (i.e., job listing, data bank service, ads for job hunters, resumé referral service, workshops, job fairs, video tapes, books, etc.). If you belong to an association or trade group, check to see what services are available. Some associations provide substantial job assistance to members. Many of these associations are industry or profession-related such as:

Electronics (American Electronics Association— AEA)

Financial (Financial Executives Institute—FEI)

Aerospace (American Institute of Aeronautics and Astronautics— AIAA)

Electrical/Electronics (Institute of Electrical and Electronic Engineers—IEEE)

Defense Electronics (Association of Old Crows—AOC)

Human Resources (Society of Human Resources Management— SHRM)

Management (American Management Association—AMA)

Women (American Business Women's Association, American Society of Professional Women)

General Business Information

Business Information Sources
Lorna M. Daniels, University of California Press, 1993

U.S. Industrial Outlook, 202/482-4356
800/553-NTIS for express delivery of report or
U.S. Department of Commerce, 202/482-2000

Where To Find Business Information
Brownstone and Curruth, John Wiley & Sons Publisher

Business Magazines

Excellent publications to refer to and read are *Advertising Age, Barrons, Business Week, Forbes, Fortune, Inc., Wall Street Journal, Investors Business Daily, Time,* and *U.S. News and World Report.* And there are others, such as: various trade and technical magazines, newspapers and association publications which can be useful when they relate to your industry/profession and interests. The annual Directories of *Fortune* and *Forbes* are also helpful.

U.S. Department Of Labor

The U.S. Department of Labor provides various useful publications and forecasts (i.e. Employment Projections and Training Data, The Dictionary of Occupational Titles [DOT]). The Bureau of Labor Statistics provides ongoing useful U.S. work force information. Projections are available for the American work force, such as the fastest growing industries, occupations adding the most jobs, and so on. More detailed information on the 1992-2005 employment projections appears within five articles of the November 1993 issue of the Monthly Labor Review, published by the Bureau of Labor Statistics, U.S. Department of Labor. A graphic presentation of these highlights of the projections appeared in the Fall 1993 Occupational Outlook Quarterly.

The Monthly Labor Review and Occupations Outlook Quarterly are sold by the U.S. Government Printing Office, Washington, D.C. 20402. Some material can be found in the public library (i.e., Occupational Outlook Handbook). For additional data contact either:

U.S. Department of Labor
Bureau of Labor Statistics
2 Massachusetts Ave., N.E., Room 2860
Washington, D.C. 20212   Telephone 202/606-5886
or
General Office of Public Affairs
200 Constitution Avenue
Washington, D.C. 20210   Telephone 202/219-7316

Reminder

Job Sources Available

- Traditional job market

- Nontraditional/behind-the-scenes job market

- Hidden job market

- Job sources to develop (networking—old and new contacts)

  - New and unknown contact sources through cold calls, inquiry and information calls

  - Sources obtained by new personal interaction/meetings with individuals, groups and associations involving leaders, managers, executives, authors, etc., in your career field and areas of interest.

  - Sources obtained through personal development, training, entrepreneurial efforts, community and volunteer activities, temporary/interim employment, network marketing, etc.

- Target companies applicable to your skills and experience

- Job-Source Information List provided in Appendix 6

- Insights from the Job Hunters' Survey (*99 Minutes,* Chapter 3, the Most Effective Sources of Job Leads/Interviews)[1]

- The Major Sources of Job-Opportunities (*99 Minutes,* Chapter 8)

- Insights from the Employers' Surveys (99 Minutes, Chapter 3) and Recruitment Sources Employers Use to Find New Hires (Chapter 7)[2]

- Also see—Effective Methods of Marketing and Selling Yourself (*99 Minutes,* Chapter 9)

---

[1] Thomas Mangum Company, *Job Hunter's Questionnaire for Executive Management, Professional, and Technical Personnel,* 1993, 1994; Thomas Mangum Company, *Job Hunter's Questionnaire for Hiring Managers,* 1994.

[2] The Employment Management Association (EMA) and Thomas Mangum Company, (TMI). *Employment Market Survey: Employer Assessment of Current/Future Employment Market for Executive, Middle Management and Professional Staff,* joint project, 1993, 1994.

Recommendation / Information Update

We would appreciate your input!

Additional job-search tools you believe are effective:

_____

_____

_____

_____

_____

Additional job sources and job-search techniques you believe are
effective:

_____

_____

_____

_____

_____

Additional comments:

_____

_____

_____

_____

_____

Please send to: TMI Publications
                 P.O. Box 50001
                 Pasadena, CA 91115-0001
                 or fax to: 818/568-0638

Thank you

Work Sheet Order Form

For job hunters wishing to use the specific work forms provided in the workbook, please check below the forms requested.

Works Forms	Exhibit #	# of Packets
___ 1. Contacts Work Sheet (all sources)	Exhibit 1.C	#_____
___ 2. Individual Job Source Work Sheet	Exhibit 1.D	#_____
___ 3. Target Company Work sheet	Exhibit 1.E.	#_____
___ 4. Telephone and Networking Work sheet Organizer (fold over)	Exhibit 1.G	#_____
___ 5. Master Organizer Work sheet	Exhibit 1.H	#_____
___ 6. 56 Potential Job Offer Items Work Sheet	Exhibit 1.G	#_____
___ 7. Full set of above listed work sheets package		#_____

Work Sheet forms available in packets of ten forms each.
a. Individual packets—$1.00 each except #4 ($2.00 each)

#_____ Total $_____
b. Full set of six packages—$5.50 per set #_____ Total $_____

CA resident tax 7-1/4% $_____
Or Los Angeles County resident tax 8-1/4%

Shipping/Handling $3.00 $_____

TOTAL AMOUNT $_____

Please send Work Sheets to:

Name_____

Address_____

_____

Signature_____

_____ VISA _____ MasterCard Expiration Date_____

Credit Card Number_____

Or make check payable to: TMI Publications
P.O. Box 50001, Pasadena, CA 91115
CALL or FAX this form to: 818/568-0638